The I ♥ TRADER JOE'S® COOKING FOR TWO COOKBOOK

99 Small-Batch Recipes Using Favorite Ingredients from the World's Greatest Grocery Store

RITA MOCK-PIKE

ULYSSES PRESS

Published by:
Ulysses Press
PO Box 3440
Berkeley, CA 94703
www.ulyssespress.com

ISBN: 978-1-64604-622-5
Library of Congress Control Number: 2023943931

Printed in China
10 9 8 7 6 5 4 3 2 1

Acquisitions editor: Kierra Sondereker
Managing editor: Claire Chun
Project editor: Paulina Maurovich
Editor: Phyllis Elving
Proofreader: Barbara Schultz
Production: Yesenia Garcia-Lopez
Artwork from shutterstock.com—*cover:* background © N_A_T_A_L_I, green beans and garlic © Nikiparonak, pan © Babich Alexander, forks © chempina, tacos © DiViArt, colander © Bodor Tivadar; *interior:* page 10 © Jan Infante; page 12 © Penny Hillcrest; page 13 © rlat; page 14 © Elena Valebnaya; pages 17, 157 © Elena Shashkina; page 19 © Olyina V; page 20 © Leron Ligred; page 23 © margouillat photo; page 25 © Andrea Skjold Mink; page 28 © Melica; page 33 © Lecker Studio; page 35 © P Maxwell Photography; page 36 © nelea33; page 39 © plamens art; page 40 © Kseniia Gorova; page 45 © siamionau pavel; page 46 © Zhanna Turetskaya; pages 52, 150 © Brent Hofacker; page 55 © YSK1; page 56 © Nadezhda Molkentin; page 59 © Ezume Images; page 60 © AVA Bitter; page 64 © MSPhotographic; page 67 © Evgenii Doljenkov; page 69 © Seva_blsv; page 70 © Rimma Bondarenko; page 72 © Vector Tradition; page 74 © Nitr; page 79 © faithie; page 81 © Rina Oshi; page 83 © Joe Gough; page 85 © JeannieR; pages 89, 97 AS Foodstudio; page 91 © Tatiana Goncharuk; pages 93, 155 © mamita; page 94 © Esin Deniz; page 101 © Lapina Maria; page 107 © PavloArt Studio; page 110 © Lubov Chipurko; page 113 © Charles Brutlag; page 115 © Olga Miltsova; page 116 © Kiian Oksana; page 119 © zi3000; page 121 © Irina Rostokina; page 122 © VasiliyBudarin; page 125 © gkrphoto; page 126 © zoryanchik; page 129 © J u n e; page 130 © Julie208; page 133 © Frances van der Merwe; page 135 © larik_malasha; page 138 © Carlota Sanz; page 140 © TinasDreamworld; page 143 © Lorraine Kourafas; page 144 © SpicyTruffel; page 147 © gowithstock; page 149 © Anna_Pustynnikova; page 151 © grafvision; page 153 © SergeyCo

Contents

PASTA DISHES 57

SEAFOOD FOR TWO 73

POULTRY DISHES FOR TWO 87

SALADS AND SOUPS 99

MEATY MAINS FOR TWO 111

DESSERTS TO SHARE 128

BEVERAGES FOR TWO 145

CONVERSIONS 158

ABOUT THE AUTHOR 159

Introduction

*H*ello young lovers and all who are young lovers at heart! I hope your cooking woes have been few and that you've clung close for companionable time together. I know my husband and I have been enjoying some delightfully delicious dates, and even more delicious foods of late.

When I was approached about doing this cookbook, another selection in the "I Love Trader Joe's!" series, I was thrilled. Cooking for two has become one of my favorite pastimes since marrying my husband, and eating that food has become one of his! And with Trader Joe ingredients, cooking is so easy—you rarely have to season or tweak anything in order to enjoy a tasty dish. But I was up for the challenge and found some amazing ways to work with TJ's already delicious selections when I wanted more than something to pop into the microwave or oven as-is.

You'll find a few semi-complicated recipes throughout this book, but ultimately my goal was to keep preparation and cooking time under 45 minutes for each recipe, and ideally under 30 minutes. You'll find many salads, wraps, and even soups that take less than 10 minutes—and loads of sandwiches, drinks, and other goodies have even shorter prep times.

I hope you'll enjoy these recipes for two, whether you're headed out on a picnic, curling up by the fireplace, or dining together before you dash out for the evening.

Breakfast

- SATURDAY MORNING CARTOONS BREAKFAST TRAY
- THE PERFECT NZ BAGEL
- PORTOBELLO QUICHE TARTS
- SAUSAGE SKILLET
- VEGETARIAN CHORIZO EGG CUPS
- HOT COCOA PANCAKES
- SAVORY SAUSAGE MUFFINS
- BLACK FOREST BACON QUICHE
- APPLE-SMOKED BACON AND EGG BISCUITS
- EVERYTHING BUT THE BAGEL BREAKFAST TARTS

SATURDAY MORNING CARTOONS BREAKFAST TRAY

You're never too old for cartoons! At least, that's the theory in our house. Every Saturday morning, my hubby and I love to snuggle up in bed and watch cartoons while we eat a hearty breakfast in bed. This easy breakfast tray is one of our favorites.

1 Trader Joe's Whole Wheat English Muffin

2 tablespoons Trader Joe's Blueberry Vanilla Chevre Cheese

2 tablespoons Trader Joe's Double Cream Amarena Cherry Goat's Milk Cheese

2 handfuls Trader Joe's Cornbread Crisps

2 handfuls Trader Joe's Triple Ginger Pretzels

1 Trader Joe's Glazed Orange Poppy Seed Scone

½ tablespoon butter

1 tablespoon jam or jelly of choice

1. Pop the English muffin halves into the toaster while you prep the rest of the tray. Adjust the toaster setting to your preferred darkness.

2. Set a platter on a tray and slice both cheeses onto the platter—about 4 slices each, about 1 tablespoon per slice. Place the cornbread crisps alongside. Next put out the pretzels and scone, cut in half.

3. When the English muffin is ready, set it on the platter, spread the butter on each half, and then add the jam or jelly. Serve immediately.

PREP TIME: 7 minutes
COOK TIME: 5 minutes
TOTAL TIME: 7 minutes

THE PERFECT NZ BAGEL

This past spring I spent several weeks in New Zealand. As I left the country, the last thing I expected to find at the airport at 10 p.m. was the most amazing bagel I've ever eaten. This delicious breakfast (or late-night snack!) was inspired by that NZ meal.

2 Trader Joe's Gluten-Free Everything Bagels

2 tablespoons Trader Joe's Vegan Cream Cheese

2 teaspoons fresh-squeezed lemon juice

dash cracked black pepper

4 large tomato slices

1 handful fresh basil leaves (optional)

2 teaspoons olive oil

1. Preheat the oven to 375°F. Open or split the bagels and place on a baking sheet, sliced side up. Smear the cream cheese on all four bagel slices. Next drizzle on the lemon juice, sprinkle on the cracked pepper, and add the tomato—one slice for each bagel half. Top with the basil leaves, if using, and drizzle with the olive oil.

2. Place the bagels in the oven and toast for 5 minutes. Remove from the oven and let stand 3 minutes, then serve.

ACTIVE TIME: 5 minutes
COOKING TIME: 5 minutes
TOTAL TIME: 10 minutes

PORTOBELLO QUICHE TARTS

I'm a huge fan of quiche—but since I live a gluten-free life, it's hard for me to find a quick, easy quiche to enjoy. That's where portobello caps come in!

4 large eggs

1 green onion, chopped, plus more, for topping

¼ cup Trader Joe's Grated Parmesan Cheese

1 teaspoon Trader Joe's Cuban Style Citrusy Garlic Seasoning Blend

4 large portobello mushroom caps

2 tablespoons Trader Joe's Organic Kansas City Style BBQ Sauce (optional)

1. Preheat the oven to 375°F. In a small bowl, with a rubber spatula, stir together the eggs, green onion, cheese, and seasoning blend. Mix thoroughly until fully combined, then set aside.

2. Lightly grease a baking sheet and set the mushroom caps on the tray, then fill them with the egg mixture.

3. Bake for 17 minutes, or until the eggs have become firm. Then remove from the oven and let cool for 2 to 3 minutes. If desired, top with the remaining chopped green onions and BBQ sauce, if using; serve immediately.

PREP TIME: 7 minutes
COOK TIME: 17 minutes
TOTAL TIME: 24 minutes

SAUSAGE SKILLET

Who needs to go to a diner when you can make your own Trader Joe's sausage skillet at home? This easy recipe is delicious and fun to eat together. I love serving it for our traditional Saturday morning "cartoons in bed" sessions.

olive oil

1 cup Trader Joe's Potato Tots, thawed

2 Trader Joe's Smoked Andouille Chicken Sausage

4 eggs

1 green pepper, chopped

2 Roma tomatoes, chopped

2 green onions, chopped

1 teaspoon Trader Joe's Cuban Style Citrusy Garlic Seasoning Blend

½ cup shredded mozzarella cheese

1. Start by oiling a large skillet with olive oil. Set on the stovetop, turn the heat to medium, and let the pan warm for about 2 minutes. Then add the potato tots and cook for about 5 minutes, stirring every couple of minutes to keep them from sticking to each other or to the pan.

2. Pierce each sausage a few times with a fork and add to the pan. Cook for about 5 minutes, turning them over about halfway through.

3. While the tots and sausages are heating up, combine the eggs, vegetables, and seasoning blend in a small bowl. Mix thoroughly with a fork.

4. Once the tots and sausages are warm, remove sausages from the pan and chop into bite-size pieces.

5. Add sausages back into the pan. Add the seasoned eggs to the pan between the sausages and tots. Using a spatula, keep stirring the eggs, veggies, sausages, and tots until the eggs begin to cook through, about 5 minutes.

6. Top the dish with the cheese and let cook for another 3 minutes, or until the cheese starts to melt. Then remove the skillet from the heat and let stand for 3 minutes. Divide the meal between two plates and serve.

PREP TIME: 7 minutes
COOKING TIME: 23 minutes
STANDING TIME: 3 minutes
TOTAL TIME: 33 minutes

VEGETARIAN CHORIZO EGG CUPS

A tasty and healthy vegetarian breakfast is the perfect way to kick off the day. Loads of protein, lots of flavor, and easy prep add up to a tasty start for your morning.

4 large eggs

¼ red onion, diced

¼ cup Trader Joe's Soy Chorizo, cooked and crumbled

1 teaspoon garlic powder

1 teaspoon chili powder

1 teaspoon ground cumin

1 tablespoon Trader Joe's Blanched Almond Flour

½ teaspoon baking soda

1. Preheat the oven to 400°F. Either place four metal or silicon muffin cups in a muffin tin or lightly grease four of the openings in the muffin tin. Set aside.

2. In a small mixing bowl, combine all the ingredients until thoroughly incorporated. Using a spoon, evenly distribute the mixture into the four muffin cups.

3. Bake the egg cups for 12 minutes, or until golden brown on top. Serve immediately.

PREP TIME: 5 minutes
COOK TIME: 12 minutes
TOTAL TIME: 17 minutes

HOT COCOA PANCAKES

Admittedly, I'm not a huge chocolate fan. But there is something about hot cocoa that always captures my imagination and taste buds. So when I wanted to whip up something extra special for my hubby—who also loves some good cocoa—I thought, why not combine it with pancakes? What better breakfast on a special day than hot cocoa pancakes?

1 cup buttermilk "just add-water" pancake mix

¼ cup dry Trader Joe's Organic Hot Cocoa Mix or Trader Joe's Peppermint Hot Chocolate Mix

½ tablespoon unsweetened cocoa powder

¾ cup water

½ teaspoon vanilla extract

suggested toppings: hot fudge sauce, whipped cream, Oreo cookie bits, chocolate chips, caramel syrup, cinnamon syrup, peppermint candy bits, whipped peanut butter, sliced bananas

1. Heat a stovetop pancake griddle to 375°F or medium heat. Lightly grease the griddle.

2. In a medium mixing bowl, combine the dry pancake mix, cocoa mix, and cocoa powder until thoroughly integrated. Add the water and vanilla and whisk until well incorporated.

3. Spoon ¼ cup batter per pancake onto the griddle. Cook for 1 to 1½ minutes, or until the tops start to bubble; the bottoms should be slightly browned. Then flip the pancakes and cook for another 1 to 1½ minutes.

4. Remove from the griddle and stack on two plates. Repeat until all the batter is used. Serve immediately with your favorite toppings.

PREP TIME: 5 minutes
COOK TIME: 2 to 3 minutes per pancake
TOTAL TIME: 17 to 23 minutes

SAVORY SAUSAGE MUFFINS

Not all muffins have to be sweet! In fact, most of my favorites are hearty versions like these savory sausage muffins. Whip them up quickly and enjoy them together as you relax over a cup of tea or get ready to work.

½ cup flour

¼ cup shredded cheese of choice

1 teaspoon dried cilantro

1 teaspoon Italian seasoning

½ teaspoon garlic powder

½ teaspoon onion powder

¼ teaspoon salt

1 teaspoon baking powder

⅓ cup buttermilk, or more as needed

1 large egg

1 teaspoon olive oil

1 link Trader Joe's Spicy Italian Chicken Sausage, diced

1. Preheat the oven to 400°F. Lightly grease 4 to 6 muffin cups, depending on your preferred muffin size, or use silicon muffin cups in a muffin tin.

2. In a medium bowl, combine the flour, cheese, seasonings, and baking powder. Stir thoroughly with a wooden spoon.

3. Add the buttermilk, egg, and olive oil and mix thoroughly until you have a chunky mixture with no dry clumps. If any dry clumps remain, add more buttermilk, 1 teaspoon at a time, until the texture is right. Lastly, mix in the diced Italian sausage; do not overmix, or the biscuits will become hard.

4. Bake for 15 minutes, or until the muffin tops are golden brown. Test with a toothpick, making sure it comes out clean before removing the muffins from the oven. Let stand for 3 to 5 minutes before serving.

PREP TIME: 5 minutes
COOK TIME: 15 minutes
TOTAL TIME: 20 minutes

BLACK FOREST BACON QUICHE

A simple, tasty quiche makes a great cook-ahead meal for a busy morning when you don't just want oatmeal or cereal. This Black Forest Bacon Quiche is pretty quick and easy to prepare, and super tasty when warmed back up again.

4 strips Trader Joe's Uncured Black Forest Bacon

4 Trader Joe's Organic Crescent Rolls dough sections

4 large eggs

½ cup shredded mozzarella cheese

¼ cup finely chopped white or yellow onion

½ teaspoon garlic powder

1 teaspoon Italian seasoning

1 teaspoon dried chives

optional toppings: sour cream, peach salsa, or BBQ sauce

1. Preheat the oven to 400°F. Line a baking sheet with parchment paper, then lay the bacon pieces side by side on the sheet. Cook for 12 to 20 minutes (12 minutes will cook the bacon, but 20 minutes will make it crisp in most cases).

2. While the bacon cooks, lightly grease two large ramekins or tart pans and set aside.

3. Lightly dust your work surface with flour. Remove two crescent roll sections from the package and ball them up together, then place on the floured work surface. Using a rolling pin, roll the dough to about a ¼-inch thickness. Divide it into two equal sections and press one section into each ramekin or tart pan, bottoms and sides, forming a "cup" of dough. Set aside.

4. Once the bacon has finished cooking, remove it from the oven. Set aside on a paper towel–lined sheet to drain. Adjust the oven temperature to 375°F.

5. In a small bowl, combine the eggs, cheese, onion, garlic powder, Italian seasoning, and dried chives. Crumble the bacon and add to the mixture. Mix with a fork until fully incorporated, then divide the mixture between the two crescent dough cups.

6. Place the ramekins into the oven and bake for 20 minutes, or until a toothpick inserted in the center comes out clean. Remove from the oven, let stand for 3 minutes, and then serve.

PREP TIME: 15 minutes
COOK TIME: 20 minutes
TOTAL TIME: 35 minutes

APPLE-SMOKED BACON AND EGG BISCUITS

For another easy breakfast choice for two, try these apple-smoked bacon and egg biscuits. You'll want to bake the biscuits ahead of time (I like to do them the night before), then cook the bacon crisp and fresh in the morning.

4 slices Trader Joe's Uncured Apple Smoked Bacon

2 large eggs

1 teaspoon garlic powder

1 teaspoon smoked paprika

1 teaspoon dried onion

2 baked Trader Joe's Organic Biscuits

½ tablespoon unsalted butter

2 slices cheddar or Swiss cheese

1. Preheat the oven to 400°F. Line a baking sheet with parchment paper, then lay the bacon pieces side by side on the sheet. Cook for 12 to 20 minutes (12 minutes will cook the bacon, but 20 minutes will make it crisp in most cases).

2. While the bacon cooks, combine the eggs, garlic powder, paprika, and dried onion in a small bowl and whisk. Lightly grease a skillet and set it on the stove over medium heat. Place two biscuit cutters in the pan, if you have them, and pour half the egg mixture into each one. If you don't have biscuit cutters, just pour the eggs directly into the skillet. Cook to the desired texture, between 3 and 7 minutes, turning the eggs, as needed, then remove the pan from the heat and set aside.

3. When the bacon is ready, transfer the pieces to a plate lined with paper towels to soak up the grease; set aside. Reduce the oven temperature to 350°F.

4. Cut the biscuits in half crosswise, place on a clean baking sheet, and pop into the oven. Warm for 3 to 5 minutes, then transfer the biscuits to two serving plates and butter them while still hot. Lay the bacon on the biscuit bottoms, then add the eggs on top. (If you didn't use biscuit cutters, simply cut the egg mixture in half and fold it on top of the bacon.) Place a cheese slice on top of the eggs and cover with the biscuit tops.

5. Serve immediately with your choice of condiments. For savory, consider Dijon mustard or BBQ sauce. For sweet, consider apple butter or a drizzle of maple syrup.

PREP TIME: 10 minutes
COOK TIME: 18 to 32 minutes
TOTAL TIME: 28 to 42 minutes

EVERYTHING BUT THE BAGEL BREAKFAST TARTS

Look no further than this for an easy, hearty breakfast meat pie. The Everything but the Bagel Sesame Seasoning Blend really brings out some extra yum in this one.

4 Trader Joe's Organic Crescent Rolls dough sections

2 teaspoons Trader Joe's Everything but the Bagel Sesame Seasoning Blend

2 tablespoons Trader Joe's Cream Cheese

1 green onion, finely chopped

1 teaspoon milk of choice

2 tablespoons Trader Joe's Pesto Rosso

1 link Trader Joe's Unexpected Cheddar Chicken Sausage, thinly sliced

1 egg white

1. Lightly grease two large (3 to 5-ounce) ramekins or tart pans and set aside. Lightly dust your work surface with flour. Remove the four crescent roll sections from the package and ball them up together, then place on the work surface. Sprinkle on the seasoning blend and work it into the dough, using your fingers.

2. Preheat the oven to 375°F. Form a third of the seasoned dough into a crust in the bottom and sides of the first ramekin or tart pan, then repeat with another third of the dough in the second one. Set aside.

3. In a small bowl, combine the cream cheese, green onion, milk, and pesto. Blend together with a fork until soft and well combined, then set aside.

4. Place the sausage slices over the dough in the ramekins or tart pans, overlapping as you go along; you will likely have some slices left over. Top with the cream cheese filling. Then divide the remaining third of the dough in half and flatten it with a rolling pin to create the tart tops. Gently press the dough tops over the tarts and pinch together with the tart sides. Prick the tops several times with a fork.

5. Lightly whisk the egg white, then brush over the tart tops. Place in the oven and bake for 20 minutes, or until the crust is golden brown. Remove from the oven and let stand for 5 minutes, then serve and enjoy!

PREP TIME: 15 minutes
COOK TIME: 20 minutes
TOTAL TIME: 35 minutes

Appetizers and Sides to Share

- RED PEPPER EGGPLANT CHICKEN DIP
- MEDITERRANEAN CHARCUTERIE
- ALL-AMERICAN CHARCUTERIE
- CITRUS GARLIC SALMON BITES
- WALNUT-STUFFED PORTOBELLOS
- POLLO ASADO BEAN DIP
- TURKEY BACON SMOKED GOUDA ROLLS
- SWEET ITALIAN SAUSAGE BITES
- APPLE-SMOKED BACON POTATO TOT BITE
- HONEY SHRIMP BRUSCHETTA

RED PEPPER EGGPLANT CHICKEN DIP

One thing I love about Trader Joe's is all the easy spreads, dips, and sauces that can be turned almost instantly into incredible appetizers and entrées. This particular offering combines several of my favorites—the plantain crisps as scoops, the eggplant–red pepper spread as the base for the dip, and cream cheese as the "filling" to make this mixture scoopable and slightly rich.

4 tablespoons Trader Joe's Eggplant Garlic Spread with Sweet Red Peppers

4 ounces unseasoned cooked light chicken, shredded

1 ounce (2 tablespoons) Trader Joe's Light Cream Cheese

½ teaspoon Trader Joe's Chile Lime Seasoning Blend

1 (5-ounce) bag Trader Joe's Plantain Crisps

1. Using a fork, combine all the ingredients except for the plantain crisps in a serving bowl. Thoroughly blend, then serve with the plantain crisps.

PREP TIME: 3 to 5 minutes

Tip: This dip tastes great made with either hot or cold chicken.

MEDITERRANEAN CHARCUTERIE

Kick back with a glass of something delightful and romantic and enjoy this simple charcuterie, inspired by one of the most romantic regions in the world—the Mediterranean! Pair it with your favorite wine, juice, or tea for the perfect evening meal for two.

½ cup pomegranate seeds

8 to 10 Trader Joe's Grilled Pitted Green Olives

4 Trader Joe's Quinoa Stuffed Dolmas

Trader Joe's Multigrain Pita Bite Crackers

2 fresh black plums

2 small bunches red or green grapes

1 ounce Trader Joe's Spanish Cheese Tapas Sampler

1 ounce Trader Joe's Italian Truffle Cheese

2 ounces Trader Joe's Sliced Prosciutto

2 ounces Trader Joe's Uncured Salame di Parma (Mild Salami)

1. Set out a charcuterie board or platter and arrange two small bowls and one medium bowl in one corner. Place the pomegranate seeds and the olives in the smaller bowls, the dolmas in the larger bowl.

2. Building out from the bowl of pomegranate seeds, add two rows of crackers. Then set a plum on either end of the board. Fill in the gap between the plums with the grapes.

3. Chop the cheeses into bite-size pieces and arrange them as the next layer outward.

4. Roll up the prosciutto slices and place alternately with the salami as the outermost row. Serve immediately.

PREP TIME: 15 minutes

ALL-AMERICAN CHARCUTERIE

While a charcuterie board may be thought of as European, there are plenty of tasty options we can use to create an all-American feast for two.

2 Pink Lady or MacIntosh apples, sliced

2 clementines, peeled and sectioned

Trader Joe's Pizza Bread Cheese

1 filet Trader Joe's Smoked Rainbow Trout Fillets

¼ cup Trader Joe's Sweet Cannoli Dip

¼ cup of your favorite hummus

1 (9.5-ounce) package Trader Joe's Jicama Sticks

4 Trader Joe's Mini Brie Bites

6 to 8 Trader Joe's Oven-Baked Cheese Bites

2 ounces Trader Joe's Uncured Salame di Parma

1. First set out a charcuterie board or platter. On a separate cutting board, slice the apples, then peel the clementines and break into sections. Cut the pizza bread cheese and the rainbow trout into bite-size pieces.

2. Place two small bowls at one corner of the charcuterie board. Fill one with the sweet cannoli dip and the other with your favorite hummus. Building outward from the bowls, lay out the fruit, alternating slices. Add a row of jicama sticks and then set out the cheese, alternating between the mini brie bites and the pizza bread cheese pieces. Add two rows of the cheese bite crackers. Finally, lay out a row of salami and then a row of smoked rainbow trout pieces. Serve immediately.

PREP TIME: 15 minutes

CITRUS GARLIC SALMON BITES

If you love appetizers as much as my husband and I do, you might find yourself making a double batch of these salmon bites and calling them dinner. They're super easy, delicious, and quick to whip up.

1 (8-ounce) package Trader Joe's Original Savory Thin Mini Crackers

4 ounces Trader Joe's Light Cream Cheese

1 (4-ounce) package Trader Joe's Oak Smoked Scottish Salmon

1 green onion, chopped

¼ teaspoon Trader Joe's Cuban Style Citrusy Garlic Seasoning Blend

small lemon edges, for garnish

1. Lay out the crackers on a serving plate or platter. Lightly spread the cream cheese on the crackers and then layer on pieces of salmon.

2. Top with the green onions and add a pinch of Citrusy Garlic seasoning to each cracker. Garnish with a small lemon wedge and serve immediately.

PREP TIME: 5 minutes

WALNUT-STUFFED PORTOBELLOS

This deliciously zingy appetizer mixes savory and sweet for a unique appetizer to enjoy together. I highly recommend pairing this with a nice salad and a meat course for a full meal.

1 (10-ounce) package Trader Joe's Baby Bella "Cremini" Mushrooms, stems removed

⅓ cup shredded Mexican-style cheese blend

2 tablespoons Trader Joe's Cream Cheese

⅓ cup walnut halves, plus more, for topping

2 green onions, chopped

1 tablespoon bread crumbs

1 teaspoon Trader Joe's Ajika Georgian Seasoning Blend

2 teaspoons Trader Joe's Dukkah Nut and Spice Blend

1. Preheat the oven to 350°F. Line a small baking sheet with parchment paper, then place the mushroom caps on the sheet. Set aside.

2. In a small mixing bowl, use a fork to mix together the cheese blend, cream cheese, walnuts, green onions, bread crumbs, and seasonings. Once thoroughly combined, use a spoon to fill the mushroom caps with the mixture.

3. Bake for 15 minutes. Then remove from the oven, let stand for 3 minutes. Top with extra walnuts and serve.

PREP TIME: 5 minutes
COOKING TIME: 15 minutes
TOTAL TIME: 20 minutes

POLLO ASADO BEAN DIP

I'm actually not a huge bean dip fan, but there's something about Trader Joe's Pollo Asada Autentico that works perfectly with black beans to create a super tasty dip. I love to serve it with plantain chips, while my hubby favors traditional corn chips. Take your pick—they're both great!

12 ounces Trader Joe's Pollo Asado Autentico, cooked and shredded

1 cup shredded Mexican or fiesta-style cheese

1 (15.5-ounce) can Trader Joe's Organic Black Beans, drained and rinsed

¼ cup milk of choice

1 teaspoon Trader Joe's Cuban Style Citrusy Garlic Seasoning Blend

1 teaspoon Trader Joe's Ajika Georgian Seasoning Blend

1 bag tortilla or plantain chips

1. Combine the shredded chicken, cheese, and black beans in a medium saucepan, stirring together thoroughly. Add the milk and seasoning blends and mix again.

2. Now turn on the stovetop burner to medium-low and cook for 4 to 5 minutes, stirring frequently. Once the cheese has begun to melt, remove the pan from the heat. Let stand for 2 or 3 minutes, then transfer to a serving bowl. Serve with the plantain or tortilla chips.

PREP TIME: 5 minutes
COOK TIME: 4 to 5 minutes
TOTAL TIME: 10 minutes

• •

Note: This recipe makes a larger batch than I'd normally recommend for two people, but it's easiest to make enough of this dip to enjoy a couple of times. And it's even better the second time around!

• •

TURKEY BACON SMOKED GOUDA ROLLS

An indulgent and amazingly yummy appetizer that goes perfectly with salads or soups, these turkey bacon rolls will keep you coming back for more. I had to limit how many I made at one time, or my husband would eat them instead of dinner!

4 uncooked Trader Joe's Organic Biscuits

olive oil for brushing the dough

2 teaspoons garlic powder

1 teaspoon smoked paprika

1 teaspoon dried oregano

¼ teaspoon ground mustard

4 to 6 strips Trader Joe's Uncured Turkey Bacon

½ cup shredded Trader Joe's Smoked Gouda

1. Preheat the oven to 375°F and line a baking sheet with parchment paper. Sprinkle your work surface with flour and use a rolling pin to roll the biscuits together. Flatten the dough into a single large, round disk. Lightly brush olive oil over the dough and then sprinkle the garlic powder, paprika, oregano, and ground mustard evenly across the surface.

2. Lay the turkey bacon strips on one side of the dough. Sprinkle on the Gouda. Then roll the dough, with the bacon and cheese inside, into a log—sort of like a Swiss roll cake, about ½ to ¾-inch thick. Using a sharp, smooth-edged knife, slice the roll up.

3. Lay the rolls on the baking sheet and pop into the oven. Bake for 17 to 20 minutes, or until the rolls are lightly browned. Remove and quickly transfer the rolls to a plate or platter. Let rest for 5 to 7 minutes before serving.

PREP TIME: 15 minutes
COOK TIME: 17 to 20 minutes
TOTAL TIME: 32 to 35 minutes

SWEET ITALIAN SAUSAGE BITES

For a bit of Seattle and Italy mixed together, try these sausage bites. Inspired by Seattle-style brats, they're flavored with Italian-style sausage and mixed with other Trader Joe offerings as appetizers. Enjoy!

½ teaspoon Trader Joe's Apple Juice

½ teaspoon grapeseed or olive oil

1 teaspoon unsalted butter

⅓ red onion, cut root to tip in thin strips

4 Trader Joe's Organic Crescent Rolls dough sections

2 tablespoons Trader Joe's Cream Cheese

1 link Trader Joe's Sweet Italian Sausage Made with Pork, cooked and cut in quarters

1. Add the apple juice, oil, and butter to a small skillet over medium-high heat, letting the mixture heat for about 1 minute. Add the cut onion and stir to coat the strips with the liquid. Spread the onion evenly over the pan and cook for about 10 minutes, stirring occasionally. If the onions appear to be burning or drying out, reduce the heat to medium or medium-low.

2. Continue cooking the onion, stirring every few minutes. You should see the onion begin to caramelize after about 20 to 30 minutes. Continue for another 5 minutes or so, or until the onion is fully caramelized. Remove from the heat and set it aside.

3. Preheat the oven to 375°F. Line a baking sheet with parchment paper and set aside. Lay out the crescent roll dough on a very lightly floured work surface. Spread ½ tablespoon cream cheese on top of each roll section. Carefully spoon about a quarter of the caramelized onion onto each section and add one sausage piece. Wrap the dough around the sausage and onions then seal and place on the baking sheet.

4. Bake for 25 to 30 minutes, or until the rolls are golden brown. Remove from the oven and let stand for 3 minutes before serving.

PREP TIME: 10 minutes
COOK TIME: 56 minutes to 1 hour 11 minutes
TOTAL TIME: 1 hour 6 minutes to 1 hour 21 minutes

APPLE-SMOKED BACON POTATO TOT BITES

Looking for a new appetizer? Try these Apple-Smoked Bacon Potato Tot Bites. They're easy and reasonably quick to make, and they offer a fun blend of spicy, sweet, and savory.

¼ cup Trader Joe's 100% Pure Maple Syrup

1 teaspoon Trader Joe's Ajika Georgian Seasoning Blend

8 strips Trader Joe's Uncured Apple Smoked Bacon

8 frozen Trader Joe's Trader Potato Tots

1. Preheat the oven to 400°F. Line a baking sheet with parchment paper and set aside.

2. In a small bowl, combine the maple syrup and Ajika seasoning. Use tongs and a fork as needed to dip each strip of bacon into the maple syrup blend. After each strip is dipped, wrap it around a potato tot and place it on the baking sheet.

3. Bake the bites for 25 to 30 minutes, until the bacon is crisp and the potato tots are tender. Serve immediately.

PREP TIME: 7 minutes
COOK TIME: 25 to 30 minutes
TOTAL TIME: 32 to 27 minutes

HONEY SHRIMP BRUSCHETTA

I thought I'd try something different for a shrimp recipe. Stumbling across the idea of a spicy honey shrimp dish, I instantly thought of a bruschetta topping—and so this delightful tangy and sweet combination was born.

4 cups plus ¼ cup water, divided

8 to 12 Trader Joe's Wild Raw Argentinian Red Shrimp

¼ cup Trader Joe's Hawaiian Macadamia Nut Blossom & Multi-Floral Honey

½ teaspoon chili powder

½ teaspoon Trader Joe's Ajika Georgian Seasoning Blend

4 Trader Joe's Everything Ciabatta Rolls, sliced open and toasted

olive oil, for brushing the ciabatta

1. Bring 4 cups of water to a boil in a medium saucepan over medium heat, about 7 to 9 minutes. Place the raw shrimp in the water and return it to a boil, another 4 to 6 minutes; leave the shrimp in the boiling water for about 3 more minutes, until thoroughly cooked. Then remove from the heat, drain the water, and set aside.

2. Preheat the oven to 375°F. Spoon the honey, ¼ cup water, chili powder, and seasoning blend into a medium bowl and stir together to combine. Then add the cooked shrimp, thoroughly coating all the shrimp and then letting them rest in the mixture.

3. Set your toasted ciabatta bread on a lightly greased baking sheet. Lightly brush the top of each slice with olive oil, then carefully place ¼ of the shrimp on each roll, letting the honey drip into the bread. Place in the oven and bake for 5 minutes, then remove and serve immediately.

COOK TIME: 19 to 23 minutes
PREP TIME: 7 minutes
TOTAL TIME: 26 to 30 minutes

Sandwiches and Wraps

- COLLARD GREEN-CHILADAS
- CUCUMBER TOMATO CROSTINI
- JICAMA CHICKEN SALAD WRAPS
- DILL-SMOKED SALMON GRILLED CHEESE
- WINE COUNTRY GRILLED CHEESE
- BAKED SWEET POTATO MEATBALL ENCHILADA WRAPS
- CHICKEN AND FRUIT SALAD TOASTED SANDWICHES
- RED PEPPER CHICKEN CRUNCH TOASTED SANDWICHES
- BEEF 'N BEAN SALSA JOES
- BBQ JACKFRUIT TACOS
- GARLIC SALMON WRAP

COLLARD GREEN-CHILADAS

Tex-Mex is always welcome in our house. But since some of us are gluten-free and get stomachaches from eating corn, I'm always on the hunt for fun alternatives to those corny wraps. In this case, I turned to collard greens—and found a great substitute.

½ pound Trader Joe's Organic Ground Beef

½ cup Trader Joe's Organic Black Beans

½ cup Mexican style shredded cheese

4 large, raw collard green leaves

3 tablespoons Trader Joe's Enchilada Sauce

1. In a medium skillet, brown the beef over medium heat, about 5 minutes. Remove from the heat and let stand while you drain and thoroughly rinse the black beans and place them in a heat-resistant mixing bowl. Stir in the beef and half the cheese. Preheat the oven to 375°F.

2. Remove the stems from the collard greens and lay the greens open on a flat surface. Spoon the beef and bean mix into the leaves without overstuffing them. Fold the leaves around the mix, flip them over, and place on a lightly greased glass baking pan.

3. Bake for 10 minutes, then remove from the oven to sprinkle on the remaining cheese and drizzle on about half of the enchilada sauce. Return the pan to the oven and bake for another 7 minutes.

4. Remove the green-chiladas from the oven and let stand for 3 minutes. Then plate them, drizzle with the remaining enchilada sauce, and serve.

ACTIVE TIME: 7 minutes
COOKING TIME: 22 minutes
TOTAL TIME: 29 minutes

CUCUMBER TOMATO CROSTINI

Crostini are among my favorite hors d'oeuvres and snacks to serve, especially when it's just the two of us. They're a great part of a platter, nibbly meal, or holiday spread, and always delicious. In this case, they're also healthy!

2 ounces Trader Joe's Burrata cheese

8 to 10 slices Trader Joe's Organic French Baguette

olive oil

1 cucumber

2 Roma tomatoes

2 green onions

4 tablespoons Trader Joe's Cilantro Salad Dressing

SPECIAL EQUIPMENT: COUNTERTOP OR CHARCOAL GRILL OR AIR FRYER

1. Before you start cooking, pull the burrata cheese out of the fridge and let it warm up to room temperature, about 30 minutes. When the cheese is ready, slice up the baguette into 1-inch thick slices, then lightly brush each slice on both sides with olive oil.

2. Using a countertop grill, charcoal grill, or air fryer, grill the bread slices for 3 to 5 minutes. Flip the slices and grill for another 2 to 3 minutes.

3. While the bread is grilling, slice your cucumber, tomatoes, and green onions. When the bread is ready, scoop burrata onto each slice, then layer on the sliced veggies. Top with a drizzle of cilantro dressing and serve immediately.

PREP TIME: 5 minutes
COOKING TIME: 5 to 8 minutes
STANDING TIME: 30 minutes
TOTAL TIME: 40 to 43 minutes

JICAMA CHICKEN SALAD WRAPS

For date nights, we love having fast, easy, and delicious goodies to nosh on. That often means wraps, sandwiches, paninis, or salads. When it comes to making a TJ's date-night spread, it's easy and delicious! Trader Joe's Jicama Wraps have become a staple in my fridge for making yummy and quick meals like this one.

4 Trader Joe's Jicama Wraps

1 handful fresh cilantro

8 tablespoons Trader Joe's Wine Country Chicken Salad

¼ teaspoon Trader Joe's Cuban Style Citrusy Garlic Seasoning Blend

1. Lay the wraps out on a serving plate or platter and arrange a quarter of the cilantro on each wrap. Then scoop approximately 2 tablespoons of Wine Country Chicken Salad onto each wrap. Top with a dash of Citrusy Garlic Seasoning Blend.

2. Fold up the wraps and skewer with toothpicks to hold the filling in place. Serve immediately.

PREP TIME: 5 minutes

DILL-SMOKED SALMON GRILLED CHEESE

Trader Joe's Dill-icious Smoked Salmon is a super treat in our household. It's perfect for charcuterie boards with a twist and for sandwiches, salads, and more. One of our favorite ways to enjoy it is paired with grilled cheese. This simple sandwich takes just 7 minutes to cook and always tastes great, whatever mood you're in.

4 slices Trader Joe's Sprouted Flourless Whole Wheat Berry Bread

1 teaspoon unsalted butter

4 slices Swiss cheese

1 (4-ounce) package Trader Joe's Dill-Icious Seasoned Cold-Smoked Salmon

1 teaspoon Trader Joe's Vegan Creamy Dill Dressing

SPECIAL EQUIPMENT: AIR FRYER OR TABLETOP GRILL (OPTIONAL)

1. Set the bread slices on your preparation surface and spread on the butter, then flip the slices over.

2. Place a slice of Swiss cheese on the unbuttered side of two of the bread slices. Divide the salmon between the two sandwiches, evenly layering it over the cheese.

3. Lightly drizzle the salad dressing over the fish, then top each sandwich with another cheese slice and the remaining bread, butter side out. Cook by one of the following methods and then serve.

Air Fryer: Place the sandwiches on a mesh or basket-style surface in the air fryer and cook for 4 minutes. Flip the sandwiches and cook for 3 more minutes. Remove from the air fryer and let cool for 2 minutes before serving.

Tabletop Grill: Preheat the tabletop grill for 5 minutes, then place the sandwiches on the hot griddle and close the lid. Cook for 3 to 5 minutes, or until the bread is toasted and the cheese has melted.

Stovetop Griddle: Lightly brush the griddle with olive oil and preheat over medium-high for 5 minutes. Place the sandwiches on the griddle and cook for 3 minutes. Flip each sandwich (I like to use tongs for this) and cook for another 3 minutes, or until golden brown on both sides.

ACTIVE TIME: 4 minutes
COOKING TIME: 7 minutes
TOTAL TIME: 11 minutes

WINE COUNTRY GRILLED CHEESE

One of my absolute all-time favorites from Trader Joe's is the Wine Country Chicken Salad. The nuts, the fruit, the dressing, the chicken—they all combine to make a perfect treat. If you're even slightly like me, you're going to love this grilled cheese made with the chicken salad.

4 slices Trader Joe's Sprouted Flourless Whole Wheat Berry Bread or Trader Joe's Gluten-Free Multigrain Bread

2 teaspoons Trader Joe's Garlic Spread-Dip

4 slices Swiss cheese

1 cup Trader Joe's Wine Country Chicken Salad

¼ Granny Smith apple, thinly sliced (optional)

SPECIAL EQUIPMENT: AIR FRYER OR TABLETOP GRILL (OPTIONAL)

1. Place all four slices of bread on your preparation surface. Using a butter knife, spread ½ teaspoon of garlic spread across each slice. Add a slice of Swiss cheese to two slices, then layer ½ cup of the Wine Country Chicken Salad onto each cheese slice. If desired, place thin apple slices on top. Add the remaining two cheese slices and top with the last two bread slices.

2. Heat the sandwiches using one of the following methods and then serve.

Air Fryer: Place the sandwiches on a mesh or basket-style surface in the air fryer and cook for 7 minutes. Remove and let cool for 2 minutes before serving.

Tabletop Grill: Preheat the grill for 5 minutes. Then place the sandwiches on the hot griddles and close the lid. Cook for 3 to 5 minutes, or until the bread is toasted and the cheese has melted.

Stovetop Griddle: Lightly brush the griddle with olive oil and preheat on medium-high heat for 5 minutes. Place the sandwiches on the griddle and cook for 3 minutes. Flip the sandwiches (I like to use tongs for this) and cook for another 3 minutes, or until golden brown on both sides.

COOK TIME: 7 minutes
ACTIVE TIME: 5 to 7 minutes
TOTAL TIME: 12 to 15 minutes

BAKED SWEET POTATO MEATBALL ENCHILADA WRAPS

Turkey meatballs are some of the best and tastiest simple foods that Trader Joe's makes. I love using them in all kinds of recipes. In this case, I felt like using them with sweet potatoes to see what I could do with that combo. These tasty enchilada wraps are the result.

8 frozen Trader Joe's Turkey Meatballs

½ cup frozen sweet potato pieces, thawed

4 large collard green leaves

½ cup shredded Mexican or fiesta-style cheese

½ cup Trader Joe's Enchilada Sauce

1. Preheat the oven to 325°F. Spread the meatballs and sweet potato chunks in a heat-resistant pan and bake for 30 minutes.

2. While the meatballs and sweet potatoes are heating, lay out the collard green leaves on your work surface. Slightly crack the spines to help flatten them. Sprinkle a quarter of the cheese on each leaf.

3. When the meatballs and sweet potatoes are done cooking, arrange the sweet potato pieces on the leaves. Then add two meatballs to each leaf and drizzle on a bit of the enchilada sauce. Fold the leaves around the filling, flip over, and skewer with toothpicks to hold the wraps together while they bake.

4. Bake the wraps for 5 minutes, then flip them using tongs. Bake for another 5 minutes, then remove from the oven and let stand for 2 minutes. Then transfer the wraps to plates, drizzle the rest of the sauce over them, and serve.

ACTIVE TIME: 7 minutes
COOKING TIME: 40 minutes
TOTAL TIME: 47 minutes

CHICKEN AND FRUIT SALAD TOASTED SANDWICHES

I absolutely love toasted sandwiches, so you might not be surprised to see another one here. This one uses a longtime favorite recipe but adds a twist—and poppyseed dressing. Yum!

½ cup cooked and shredded chicken breast

¼ cup halved red grape

1 handful fresh cilantro, stemmed and chopped

1 tablespoon unsalted sunflower kernels

4 teaspoons Trader Joe's Organic Poppy Seed Dressing, or to taste

4 slices Trader Joe's Sprouted Flourless Whole Wheat Berry Bread or Trader Joe's Gluten-Free Multigrain Bread

1 teaspoon unsalted butter

2 teaspoons Trader Joe's Garlic Spread-Dip

4 slices Gouda cheese

SPECIAL EQUIPMENT: AIR FRYER, TABLETOP GRILL, OR STOVETOP GRIDDLE

1. In a small mixing bowl, use a fork to combine the shredded chicken breast, grape halves, cilantro, sunflower kernels, and poppyseed dressing. Set aside.

2. Place the bread slices on your preparation surface and slather butter on all four slices, then flip the bread over and spread ½ teaspoon of the garlic spread across each slice. Place a slice of Gouda cheese over the garlic spread on two bread slices, then layer on the homemade chicken salad. Top with the other two cheese slices and the remaining bread slices, buttered sides on top.

3. Heat your sandwiches by one of the following methods, then serve.

Air Fryer: Place the sandwiches on a mesh or basket-style surface in the air fryer. Cook for 4 minutes at 375°F, then flip and cook for another 3 minutes. Remove from the air fryer and let cool for 2 minutes before serving.

Tabletop Grill: Preheat the tabletop grill for 5 minutes to 350°F. When the grill is ready, place the sandwiches on the hot griddle and close the lid. Cook for 3 to 5 minutes, or until the bread is toasted and the cheese has melted.

Stovetop Griddle: Lightly brush the griddle with olive oil and preheat the griddle on the stove for 5 minutes to medium-high heat. Place the sandwiches on the griddle and cook for 3 minutes. Flip each sandwich (I like to use tongs for this) and cook for another 3 minutes, or until golden brown on both sides.

PREP TIME: 4 minutes
COOKING TIME: 7 minutes
TOTAL TIME: 11 minutes

RED PEPPER CHICKEN CRUNCH TOASTED SANDWICHES

As a huge fan of Trader Joe's Red Pepper with Eggplant and Garlic Spread, I'm constantly on the lookout for ways to use this delicious, hearty spread. When I find one, my excitement may be a little over the top—but in this case it's well founded. The spread makes the perfect topping for a chicken sandwich you'll not soon forget.

1 tablespoon olive oil

8 ounces canned chicken

4 tablespoons Trader Joe's Red Pepper with Eggplant and Garlic Spread

¼ teaspoon Trader Joe's Chili Onion Crunch

4 slices multigrain bread

4 slices Muenster cheese

1. Preheat your oven or air fryer to 375°F. Empty the canned chicken into a strainer and thoroughly rinse. Shred the meat with a fork, if it isn't already fine enough, and place it in a medium bowl. Mix in the red pepper eggplant spread, dribble in the crunchy chili, and combine thoroughly.

2. Lay out the bread slices on a plate and top with the cheese. Layer the chicken mixture on two of the bread slices, then cover with the remaining two slices, cheese-side down. Slide the sandwiches into the oven or air fryer directly onto the rack and heat for 5 to 7 minutes.

• •

Tip: Double the amount of Crunchy Chili Onion if you want a bit more of a kick!

• •

COOK TIME: 7 minutes
ACTIVE TIME: 5 to 7 minutes
TOTAL TIME: 12 to 14 minutes

BEEF 'N BEAN SALSA JOES

I was feeling the need for a good, messy sandwich one day but didn't have the supplies on hand for a traditional Sloppy Joe. So, I thought, why not go Tex-Mex? The result was one of the most delicious and messiest meals I've had in a long time!

8 ounces Trader Joe's Organic Ground Beef

½ cup canned Trader Joe's Organic Black Beans

½ cup Trader Joe's Salsa Autentica

1 teaspoon Trader Joe's Chile Lime Seasoning Blend

1 teaspoon garlic powder

1 teaspoon dried minced onion

2 whole wheat hamburger buns

2 slices cheddar cheese (optional)

1. Over medium heat, brown the ground beef in a medium skillet until it is thoroughly cooked. While the meat cooks, drain the liquid from the black beans and rinse them thoroughly with a colander.

2. Drain the fat from the cooked ground beef and place the meat in a medium bowl. Add the salsa. seasoning blend, garlic powder, and dried onion along with the black beans. Mix until well combined.

3. Put a hamburger bun on each plate. If using, add a slice of cheese on the bottom of each bun. Cover the cheese with the meat and bean mix, cover with the top bun, and serve immediately.

COOK TIME: 7 to 10 minutes
ACTIVE TIME: 7 minutes
TOTAL TIME: 14 to 17 minutes

BBQ JACKFRUIT TACOS

My husband has about seven primary food groups—and tacos are one of them. Whenever I find a new way to create tasty Tex-Mex, he's thrilled. The fact that these BBQ Jackfruit Tacos are a bit healthier than many options doesn't hurt, either.

4 cups water

1 (10-ounce) package Trader Joe's Pulled Jackfruit in Smoky BBQ Sauce

1 box Trader Joe's Organic Stone Ground Yellow Corn Taco Shells

2 or 3 mustard green leaves

½ cup shredded Mexican-style cheese

2 Trader Joe's Fire Roasted Red Peppers, diced

¼ cup shredded carrot (optional)

4 thin slices fresh, firm avocado (optional)

¼ cup shredded cabbage (optional)

1. Bring the water to a boil over medium-high heat in a medium saucepot and insert the sealed jackfruit as directed on the package. Cook for 5 minutes.

2. While the jackfruit cooks, lay out the organic stone ground yellow corn taco shells. Strip the leafy parts of the mustard greens from the stem, then arrange them lightly on the shells.

3. Remove the jackfruit package from the boiling water and set aside. Sprinkle the cheese on the mustard greens, then use a fork to layer the still-hot jackfruit over the cheese to help it melt. Add the diced red peppers on top, and serve. You can additionally add carrots, avocado, and shredded cabbage, if desired.

ACTIVE TIME: 7 minutes
COOKING TIME: 5 minutes
TOTAL TIME: 12 minutes

GARLIC SALMON WRAP

Wraps and sandwiches are perfect picnic foods. And what says romance better than a spontaneous getaway from the workday as you surprise your partner with a front lawn picnic on some random Monday? These little wraps are perfect for just such an occasion.

4 Trader Joe's Jicama Wraps

1 tablespoon Trader Joe's Garlic Spread-Dip

1 (4-ounce) package Trader Joe's Oak Smoked Scottish Salmon

1 green onion

1. Spread out the jicama wraps on your preparation surface. Spread roughly ¼ tablespoon garlic dip on each wrap, then layer on about a quarter of the salmon on each wrap. Top with the chopped green onion.

2. Fold the jicama around the filling and skewer with toothpicks to hold the wraps together. Serve immediately, or chill for an hour to let everything "soak in" and spread flavor.

PREP TIME: 4 minutes
CHILLING TIME: 1 hour (optional)
TOTAL 4 minutes or 1 hour 4 minutes

Pasta Dishes

- LOBSTER MAC 'N CHEESE
- ALMOND PESTO CHICKEN PASTA
- PESTO HAM SEDANINI 'N CHEESE
- CREAMY BEEF 'N CHEESE PENNE PASTA
- CHEESY LIMONE ALFREDO ZOODLE DELIGHT
- CHICKEN PESTO SEDANINI
- FIRE-ROASTED CHILI CHICKEN PASTA SALAD
- CHICKEN LIMONE ALFREDO
- CAULIFLOWER GNOCCHI BOWL
- TURKEY VEGETABLE MARINARA KOHLRABI PASTA

LOBSTER MAC 'N CHEESE

For our wedding, we had a mac 'n cheese bar for the main course at the reception. So now we think back to that special day every time we eat mac 'n cheese. This meal remains one of our favorites, and mixing it up with different cheeses and toppings keeps it fresh for us. This version is a new favorite!

4 cups water

dash of salt (optional)

1⅓ cups macaroni noodles

2 tablespoons milk of choice

4 ounces cream cheese

½ cup shredded Swiss cheese

1 teaspoon garlic powder

1 teaspoon ground rosemary

1 teaspoon ground thyme

½ teaspoon smoked paprika

1 (12-ounce) package Trader Joe's Langostino Tails, thawed

1. Add the water to a medium saucepot; add a dash of salt if desired. Bring the water to a boil, about 7 minutes, and then add the pasta. Stir a few times to break up the clumps, bring back to a boil, and cook for about 8 minutes, stirring occasionally.

2. Remove the noodles from the heat, drain, and return them to the saucepot. Add the milk, then the cream cheese and Swiss cheese. Bring back to medium-low heat and stir constantly until the cheese, milk, and pasta blend together smoothly, about 3 minutes. Once the cheese has melted, add the seasonings. Stir to combine, then remove the pan from the heat.

3. Plate your mac 'n cheese and top with the Langostino tails and serve immediately.

ACTIVE TIME: 5 minutes
COOKING TIME: 18 minutes
TOTAL TIME: 23 minutes

ALMOND PESTO CHICKEN PASTA

Pasta is always popular in our household—especially since we've discovered healthier, gluten-free options such as brown rice penne. These are now my go-to noodles, and I use them for just about everything. Top them with incredible sauces such as pesto and you can't lose.

4 cups water

dash of salt (optional)

1⅓ cups uncooked Trader Joe's Organic Brown Rice Penne Pasta

½ cup Trader Joe's Organic Roasted Red Pepper and Almond Pesto Sauce

8 ounces cooked, shredded chicken breast

1 cucumber, peeled and diced

½ teaspoon Trader Joe's Italian Style Soffritto Seasoning Blend

1. Add the water to a medium saucepot, then add a dash of salt, if desired. Bring the water to a boil over medium-high heat, about 7 minutes. Add the pasta and stir a few times to break up the clumps. Bring back to a boil and cook, stirring occasionally, for about 8 minutes, then remove from the heat. Drain the pasta thoroughly and rinse lightly, then set aside.

2. In a small bowl, combine the remaining ingredients so that the chicken and cucumber are thoroughly coated with the pesto sauce and seasoning blend. Divide the pasta between two dinner plates, then top with the chicken-pesto sauce. Serve immediately.

PREP TIME: 7 minutes
COOKING TIME: 15 minutes
TOTAL TIME: 22 minutes

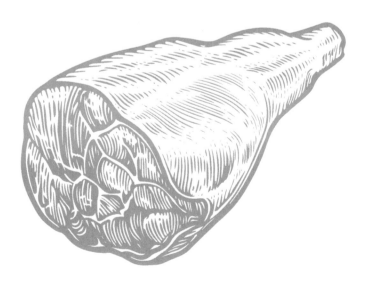

PESTO HAM SEDANINI 'N CHEESE

There's nothing more exciting in our household than a good batch of mac and cheese. We've tried dozens of variations and have loved almost all of them. But when I whipped up this dish, my husband asked when we would have it again—hoping it would be the next meal!

3 cups water

1½ cups uncooked Trader Joe's Organic Red Lentil Sedanini

⅛ cup unsweetened almond milk (or other unsweetened milk)

½ cup shredded Mexican-style cheese

4 ounces cooked or uncured ham, chopped or cubed

1 tablespoon Trader Joe's Organic Roasted Red Pepper and Almond Pesto Sauce

1 cup chopped fresh spinach

1. In a medium saucepan, bring 3 cups of water to a boil over medium-high heat. When the water is boiling, add the sedanini pasta and stir immediately to prevent the noodles from clumping. Bring back to a boil, stirring occasionally, about 5 to 6 minutes. When the noodles reach the boiling point, they should be tender but not squishy.

2. Remove the noodles from the stovetop and drain. Return them to the pot and pour in the milk, stirring it in thoroughly. Next sprinkle the cheese evenly over the noodles and use a wooden spoon to stir it in.

3. Turn the heat back on at medium-low, return the pan to the stove, and add the ham with the noodles, stirring to blend. Once the cheese is melted and stringy, stir in the pesto sauce and chopped spinach. Turn off the heat as you finish combining the ingredients. Let stand for 2 minutes and then serve.

CREAMY BEEF 'N CHEESE PENNE PASTA

Sometimes you need something warming and beefy to set the right mood for a relaxed evening with your loved one. Pasta does the trick for me and my hubby—so this dish is perfect. Cuddle up before the fire with a bowlful for a perfect, cozy night.

4 cups water

dash of salt (optional)

1⅓ cups Trader Joe's Organic Brown Rice Penne Pasta, uncooked

½ pound Trader Joe's Organic Ground Beef

¼ cup low-fat milk

½ cup shredded Mexican-style cheese

1 teaspoon garlic powder

1 teaspoon dried rosemary

1 teaspoon dried minced onion

1 teaspoon Italian seasoning

1 teaspoon Trader Joe's Chile Lime Seasoning Blend

1. Add the water to a medium saucepot; add a dash of salt, if desired. Bring the water to a boil over medium-high heat, about 7 minutes. Add the pasta and stir a few times to break up any clumps. Bring back to a boil and cook, stirring occasionally, for about 8 minutes. Then remove from the heat, drain thoroughly, rinse lightly, and set aside.

2. While the pasta is cooking, use a medium skillet to brown the beef over medium-high heat for about 5 minutes. Remove from the heat, drain off any fat, and set aside.

3. Add the beef to the drained pasta in the saucepot, then add all the remaining ingredients. Mix thoroughly, then fill your dinner bowls and enjoy immediately.

ACTIVE TIME: 7 minutes
COOKING TIME: 20 minutes
TOTAL TIME: 27 minutes

CHEESY LIMONE ALFREDO ZOODLE DELIGHT

Not all pasta is made of dough. In this case, zoodles steal the show with a tasty, unique twist on an alfredo dish.

4 to 6 frozen Trader Joe's Turkey Meatballs

1 (12-ounce) frozen box Trader Joe's Trader Joe's Zucchini Spirals

½ cup shredded Romano cheese

¼ cup fresh tomato, sliced

1½ cups Trader Joe's Limone Alfredo Sauce

1. Preheat the oven to 325°F. Spread the meatballs on a heat-resistant pan and bake for 30 minutes.

2. After the meatballs have been heating for about 20 minutes, follow the directions on the zucchini spirals package and cook the noodles—either in the microwave (4 to 5 minutes) or by sautéing them on the stovetop (5 minutes). Personally, I prefer to sauté.

3. Divide the shredded cheese between two plates. Once the noodles are cooked, immediately spread them on the beds of cheese.

4. Spoon the Limone Alfredo Sauce evenly across both plates, then add the tomatoes. Remove the meatballs from the oven and top each plate with two or three meatballs.

PREP TIME: 5 minutes
COOKING TIME: 35 minutes
TOTAL TIME: 40 minutes

CHICKEN PESTO SEDANINI

Pesto sauce is one of those things that makes any Italian-style meal better. Red Pepper and Almond Pesto Sauce is a favorite around here, particularly in pasta dishes. For this recipe, you need just a little of the pesto and some cream cheese, chicken, and pasta to make one of the tastiest and fastest meals around. Thank you, Trader Joe's!

4 cups water

dash of salt (optional)

1½ cups Trader Joe's Organic Red Lentil Sedanini, uncooked

8 to 10 strips Trader Joe's Grilled Chicken Strips, thawed

4 tablespoons Trader Joe's Organic Roasted Red Pepper and Almond Pesto Sauce

1 teaspoon milk of choice

2 ounces Trader Joe's Cream Cheese

1 teaspoon Trader Joe's Cheesy Seasoning Blend

1. Pour the water into a medium saucepot; add a dash of salt, if desired. Bring the water to a boil over medium-high heat, about 7 minutes, then add the pasta and stir a few times to break up the clumps. Bring back to a boil and cook, stirring occasionally, for about 8 minutes.

2. While the pasta is cooking, lightly oil a cast-iron skillet and let it warm for 3 minutes over medium heat. Then add the chicken strips and cook for 4 minutes, turning them over with tongs after about 2 minutes. Mix the pesto sauce, milk, cream cheese, and seasoning blend in a small bowl and then add to the chicken strips. Combine thoroughly, then remove from heat.

3. When the pasta is done cooking, drain and rinse lightly with warm water. Divide it between two dinner plates or bowls, then top with the pesto sauce mixture and warmed chicken strips. Enjoy!

PREP TIME: 5 minutes
COOK TIME: 15 minutes
TOTAL TIME: 20 minutes

FIRE-ROASTED CHILI CHICKEN PASTA SALAD

Pasta salad makes the perfect date food, in my opinion! It's easy and quick to make ahead and works perfectly for a lovely picnic in the park or a fireside meal in the living room.

4 cups water

dash of salt (optional)

1⅓ cups uncooked Trader Joe's Organic Brown Rice Penne Pasta

8 to 10 Trader Joe's Grilled Chicken Strips, thawed and cubed

1 teaspoon Trader Joe's Crunchy Chili Onion

1 cup Trader Joe's Organic Baby Spinach

¼ cup Trader Joe's Vegan Caesar Dressing

2 Trader Joe's Fire Roasted Red Peppers, diced

1. Add the water to a medium saucepot; add a dash of salt, if desired. Bring the water to a boil, about 7 minutes. Add the pasta and stir a few times to break up the clumps. Bring back to a boil and cook about 8 minutes, stirring occasionally, then remove from the heat.

2. Drain the pasta and rinse lightly with cool water, then transfer it to a medium bowl and add all the remaining ingredients. Mix to coat everything with the dressing, then cover and chill in the refrigerator for 4 to 6 hours before serving.

PREP TIME: 5 minutes
COOK TIME: 15 minutes
REST TIME: 4 to 6 hours
TOTAL TIME: 4 hours 20 minutes to 6 hours 20 minutes

CHICKEN LIMONE ALFREDO

If the two of you want to cuddle up over a romantic Italian-style meal inspired by flavor and fueled by love, you're in luck. Trader Joe's Limone Alfredo Sauce supplies you with all the elegance and flavor you could want, while the chicken adds that extra something to make the evening perfect.

4 cups water

dash of salt (optional)

1⅓ cups uncooked Trader Joe's Organic Brown Rice Penne Pasta

1 cup Trader Joe's Limone Alfredo Sauce

8 to 10 Trader Joe's Grilled Chicken Strips, thawed

1 cup broccoli

2 dashes Trader Joe's Italian Style Soffritto Seasoning Blend

1. Add the water to a medium saucepot; add a dash of salt, if desired. Bring the water to a boil, about 7 minutes, then add the pasta and stir a few times to break up the clumps. Bring back to a boil and cook, stirring occasionally, for about 8 minutes. Then remove from the heat, drain the pasta, and rinse lightly with warm water.

2. While the pasta is cooking, place the Limone Alfredo Sauce and chicken in a small saucepan and warm over medium heat for about 5 minutes. Stir to cover the chicken with the sauce.

3. Divide the pasta evenly between two dinner plates or bowls. Top with the warmed sauce and chicken, add the broccoli and sprinkle each serving with a dash of Soffritto seasoning. Serve immediately.

PREP TIME: 5 minutes
COOK TIME: 15 minutes
TOTAL TIME: 20 minutes

CAULIFLOWER GNOCCHI BOWL

I'm a big fan of bowl meals. They're easy to serve and clean up, and there's just something comforting about holding a bowl of good grub as you sit with your true love watching a great movie. This bowl meal is a little different, with some scrummy gnocchi and enough arugula to give it a mildly spicy kick.

1 (12-ounce) package Trader Joe's Cauliflower Gnocchi

4 cups water

1 cup Trader Joe's Traditional Marinara Sauce

½ cup shredded cheddar cheese

1 teaspoon Trader Joe's Italian Style Soffritto Seasoning Blend

1 teaspoon Trader Joe's Dukkah Nut and Spice Blend

1. Place your gnocchi in a medium saucepan, add the water, and stir with a wooden spoon to break free any gnocchi sticking to the bottom or each other. Turn on the heat to medium-high and bring the gnocchi to a boil, about 7 minutes.

2. Layer about ¼ cup marinara sauce in two large dinner bowls, then set aside. In a separate small bowl, mix together the Soffritto and Dukkah seasoning blends.

3. When the gnocchi has boiled, remove from the heat and immediately strain out the gnocchi with a slotted spoon. Place half in each serving bowl. Top each bowl with ¼ cup cheese, ¼ cup marinara sauce, and half of the seasoning blends mix. Serve immediately.

ACTIVE TIME: 9 minutes
COOKING TIME: 7 minutes
TOTAL TIME: 16 minutes

TURKEY VEGETABLE MARINARA KOHLRABI PASTA

Alternative noodles always intrigue me, especially when they're made from vegetables. They're especially good to use with an otherwise heavy dish, like meatball marina. In this case, they make for the perfect light touch for two in an Italian-style dish full of veggies and tomatoes.

4 to 6 frozen Trader Joe's Turkey Meatballs

1 (10-ounce) package Trader Joe's Kohlrabi Vegetable Pasta

grapeseed or olive oil for sautéing (optional)

1 cup Trader Joe's Tomato Basil Marinara Sauce

2 green bell peppers, diced

¼ yellow onion, diced

½ teaspoon garlic powder

½ teaspoon Trader Joe's Italian Style Soffritto Seasoning Blend

¼ cup Trader Joe's Shredded Lite Mozzarella Cheese

1 large tomato, diced

1. Preheat the oven to 325°F. Spread the meatballs on a baking sheet and bake for 30 minutes.

2. When the meatballs have 10 minutes left to finish cooking, follow the directions on the kohlrabi pasta package and cook the noodles in either the microwave (4 to 5 minutes) in a heat-resistant, microwave-safe bowl or by sautéing them in grapeseed or olive oil in a skillet over medium heat (about 5 minutes). I prefer to sauté for the flavor and firmer texture.

3. When the noodles are done, add the sauce, diced pepper and onion, garlic powder, and Soffritto seasoning blend to the skillet and cook for another 5 minutes. Then divide the pasta and sauce between two dinner plates. Remove the meatballs from the oven and top the pasta with the meatballs, cheese, and diced tomato.

PREP TIME: 7 minutes
COOK TIME: 30 minutes
TOTAL TIME: 37 minutes

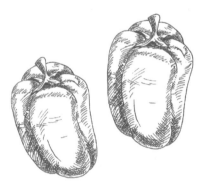

Seafood for Two

EASY SEAFOOD STIR FRY

I first mastered chopsticks when I was about four years old because my family ate stir fry nearly every week. Today I still love stir fry and getting out those sticks to enjoy a tasty Asian-inspired meal. Even better, though, is a quick and easy stir fry made from Trader Joe's delectable ingredients.

1 (16-ounce) package Trader Joe's frozen Asian Style Vegetables with Stir Fry Sauce

6 cups water

1 (16-ounce) package soba noodles

1 tablespoon grapeseed or olive oil

1 teaspoon sesame seed oil

10 to 12 ounces raw shrimp

¼ cup Trader Joe's 100% Pineapple Juice

sesame seeds, for garnish (optional)

1. Place the vegetable stir fry sauce, still sealed, in a small bowl filled with cold water. Let the sauce thaw out while you cook.

2. Add the 6 cups water to a large saucepan over medium heat. Bring to a boil, about 7 minutes, and then add the soba noodles and vegetables. Return to a boil, cook 4 or 5 minutes, and remove from the heat.

3. While the noodles and veggies are cooking, add the oils to a large skillet and warm for 3 minutes over medium heat. Add the shrimp and cook for 2 to 3 minutes, then use tongs to flip the shrimp and cook for another 2 to 3 minutes. Stir in the pineapple juice and cook for 1 or 2 more minutes.

4. Strain the noodles and vegetables with a slotted spoon and add them to the skillet. Stir everything together with a wooden spoon for 2 to 3 minutes and then add the stir fry sauce. Stir until everything is well coated. Cook for another 2 or 3 minutes, then remove from the heat and serve—chopsticks optional!

PREP TIME: 5 minutes
COOK TIME: 23 to 29 minutes
TOTAL TIME: 28 to 34 minutes

EASY DILLY SALMON BITES

Want a new go-to for a quick, flavor-packed date-night snack? These easy dill-flavored salmon bites use just a few simple ingredients and taste amazing! They're perfect for game night or casual movie nights.

4 Trader Joe's Organic Crescent Rolls dough sections

2 tablespoons sour cream

1 (4-ounce) package Trader Joe's Dill-Icious Seasoned Cold-Smoked Salmon, shredded

½ package Trader Joe's Organic Baby Spinach, shredded

1. Preheat the oven to 375°F. Line a baking sheet with parchment paper and set aside. Lightly flour a work surface and set out the four crescent roll pieces. Using a butter knife, cut each piece in half lengthwise.

2. Spread a small amount of sour cream on top of each half, then add shredded spinach. Next divide the salmon equally among the roll pieces.. Then wrap the salmon and toppings in the crescent dough.

3. Place the bites on the baking sheet, making sure they're not touching each other. Bake for 17 to 20 minutes, or until the rolls turn golden brown. Remove from the oven and let stand for 3 to 5 minutes, then serve.

PREP TIME: 5 to 7 minutes
COOK TIME: 17 to 20 minutes
TOTAL TIME: 22 to 27 minutes

SMOKED SALMON QUINOA 'N CHEESE

Using one of Trader Joe's smoked salmon offerings, this recipe is a surprisingly delicious way to pack in lean protein while keeping things gluten-free and loading up on flavor. Be sure to shred the salmon well to help it spread through the dish evenly, letting both of you enjoy the goodness.

2 cups water

1 cup uncooked quinoa

2 tablespoons milk of choice, or more as needed

½ cup shredded mozzarella cheese

½ teaspoon ground thyme

¼ teaspoon ground mustard

1 teaspoon minced dried onion

1 teaspoon garlic powder

½ teaspoon smoked paprika

1 teaspoon dried oregano

1 cup chopped baby spinach

1 (3-ounce) package Trader Joe's Oak Smoked Scottish Salmon, shredded

1. Combine the water and quinoa in a medium saucepan and bring to a boil over medium-high heat. Decrease the heat to low for a gentle simmer after the boiling point has been reached. Stir, then adjust the heat to low and let stand for 10 to 15 minutes, or until the quinoa has absorbed all the water. Remove the pan from the heat and fluff the quinoa with a fork or rigid spoon.

2. Add the milk and shredded cheese to the cooked quinoa and stir together, coating the quinoa and letting the cheese melt in. Next sprinkle in the thyme, ground mustard, onion, garlic powder, paprika, and oregano along with the chopped spinach. Stir thoroughly to combine all the ingredients. If needed, add more milk for moisture.

3. Add the shredded salmon, stirring to combine well, and serve immediately.

• •

Tip: If you find the dish a bit dry, stir in additional milk a tablespoon at a time until the desired texture is achieved.

• •

COOK TIME: 7 minutes
STAND TIME: 10 to 15 minutes
ACTIVE TIME: 7 minutes
TOTAL TIME: 24 to 29 minutes

EASY CHEESY SALMON PIE

Loosely inspired by the French-Canadian salmon pie traditionally served on Christmas and New Year's Eve, this easy version is super tasty and rich, with the bonus of cream cheese and brie mixed in. Count on leftovers, as it isn't really practical to make a quarter-size pie. Enjoy!

1 package Trader Joe's frozen Pie Crusts, thawed

2 cups Trader Joe's frozen Mashed Potatoes, thawed

1 tablespoon butter, melted

2 green onions, finely chopped

1 teaspoon dried thyme

1 teaspoon dried Italian seasoning

½ teaspoon salt

½ teaspoon ground black pepper

1 cup milk of choice

¼ wedge Trader Joe's Saint André Triple Crème Brie, softened

2 tablespoons Trader Joe's Cream Cheese, softened

1 (14.75-ounce) can red salmon, drained

1. Preheat the oven to 400°F. Line a deep-dish pie pan with one of the pie crusts. Set the second crust aside.

2. In a medium bowl, use a fork to mash together the potatoes, butter, onions, seasonings, and milk. Scoop in the brie and cream cheese and mix thoroughly, using a wooden spoon. Then mix in the salmon.

3. Spoon the potato-salmon mixture into the pie crust and then top with the second crust. Seal the crust edges together, using your fingers or a fork, and trim the excess crust edge. Cut slits in the top crust. Bake on the lower rack of the oven for 45 minutes, or until the crust is golden brown. Refrigerate leftovers in an airtight container for no more than 2 days.

PREP TIME: 10 to 13 minutes
COOK TIME: 45 minutes
TOTAL TIME: 55 to 58 minutes

INDULGENT CHEESY SHRIMP DIP

If you're looking for a super-simple, creamy, indulgent dip for date night, you've found it here! This Cheesy Shrimp Dip makes the perfect appetizer, side dish, snack food, or treat.

½ cup Trader Joe's Cream Cheese

1 tablespoon milk of choice

2 tablespoons sour cream

1 teaspoon garlic powder

1 teaspoon onion powder

1 ounce smoked Gouda

1 teaspoon white wine

½ wedge Trader Joe's Saint André Triple Crème Brie, peeled

8 to 12 frozen Trader Joe's Wild Raw Argentinian Red Shrimp, cooked and chopped into chunks

Trader Joe's Organic Garlic Naan Crackers or Trader Joe's Cauliflower Crisps

1. Combine all the ingredients except the crackers in a small saucepan and cook over medium heat for 5 to 6 minutes, or until the cheese is melted and smoothly combined.

2. Remove from the heat, transfer to a serving bowl, and offer immediately with the crackers; or cover and chill in the refrigerator for an hour and then serve.

PREP TIME: 3 to 4 minutes
COOK TIME: 5 to 6 minutes
TOTAL TIME: 8 to 10 minutes

SWEET AND SPICY SHRIMP CIABATTA ROLLS

For a quick snack or a light meal on the go, these shrimpy ciabatta rolls are the best! I love eating them either hot and fresh or cold. In other words, they're perfect for whatever kind of day we're having.

olive oil

8 to 12 frozen Trader Joe's Wild Raw Argentinian Red Shrimp, thawed

1 tablespoon Trader Joe's Hawaiian Macadamia Nut Blossom & Multi-Floral Honey, or more as needed

1 teaspoon Trader Joe's Ajika Georgian Seasoning Blend

4 pack of Trader Joe's Everything Ciabatta Rolls

2 slices Trader Joe's Sliced Provolone Cheese, cut in half

1. Lightly oil a cast-iron skillet with olive oil and set on the stovetop over medium-high heat. While the pan is heating (about 5 minutes), combine the shrimp, honey, and seasoning blend in a medium bowl. Mix with a wooden spoon to coat the shrimp thoroughly. If needed, add a teaspoon of honey for additional coating.

2. Using tongs, transfer the shrimp to the skillet. Cook for 3 minutes, then flip and cook for another 2 to 3 minutes. Remove from the heat and set aside.

3. Divide the ciabatta rolls between two plates and cut them in half. Arrange a half piece of provolone on four ciabatta halves (two per plate). Using tongs, place the shrimp on the cheese, then top with the other half of each roll. Serve immediately.

PREP TIME: 7 minutes
COOK TIME: 5 to 6 minutes
TOTAL TIME: 12 to 13 minutes

EASY "CHEAT" GLUTEN-FREE SHRIMP PAELLA

Paella! I grew up eating this wonderful dish because my parents had spent some time in Spain before I was born. But because it's so time-consuming, I rarely made it—that is, until I discovered Trader Joe's Spanish-style Rice. Now I use that and gluten-free breaded shrimp to make a "cheat" paella that's fabulously tasty without taking a long time to cook.

2 tablespoons olive oil

½ yellow onion, finely diced

½ red bell pepper, finely diced

1 clove garlic, minced

1 (20-ounce) package Trader Joe's Spanish Style Rice, thawed

2 Roma tomatoes, finely diced

1 pinch saffron threads

1 teaspoon smoked paprika

¼ teaspoon salt

¼ teaspoon ground black pepper

½ cup chicken or vegetable stock

1 (12-ounce) package Trader Joe's Gluten-Free Breaded Shrimp, thawed

1. Add the olive oil to a large skillet and place on the stove over medium heat. Warm the oil for about 1 minute, then add the onion, bell pepper, and garlic. Stir thoroughly and cook until the onion turns translucent, about 12 minutes, stirring occasionally.

2. Next, add the Spanish rice, tomatoes, saffron, paprika, salt, and pepper, and stock. Cook for 2 to 3 minutes, then add the shrimp. Cook for 4 to 5 minutes, until the shrimp is hot.

3. Reduce the heat to low, cover the pan, and let the dish simmer for 15 minutes. Remove from the heat and serve immediately.

PREP TIME: 10 minutes
COOK TIME: 34 to 36 minutes
TOTAL TIME: 44 to 46 minutes

SMOKED GOUDA SHRIMP MAC BAKE

I'm like pretty much any other American in that mac 'n cheese is one of my absolute favorite dishes! There's something so cozy and comforting about this creamy, cheesy concoction. Even better is when you can add some shrimp and seasoning for an extra bit of delight. Then, of course, adding even more cheese—well, you really can't beat it!

1 (12-ounce) package Trader Joe's Gluten Free Mac & Cheese or 1 (14-ounce) package Joe's Diner Four Cheese Mac 'n Cheese, thawed

1 (9-ounce) package Trader Joe's Argentinian Red Shrimp with Ginger Garlic Butter, thawed

¼ cup shredded smoked Gouda cheese

2 tablespoons milk of choice

1 teaspoon garlic powder

1 teaspoon onion powder

1 teaspoon smoked paprika

¼ cup Trader Joe's Organic Bread Crumbs

1. Preheat the oven to 375°F. Lightly grease a 9 x 9-inch baking pan, then scoop the mac 'n cheese into the pan. Arrange the shrimp on top as evenly as you can, then sprinkle on the shredded Gouda.

2. Pour the milk, garlic powder, onion powder, and paprika into a small jar with a watertight lid and shake vigorously to combine. Pour the mixture over the mac 'n cheese and then scatter the bread crumbs on top.

3. Loosely cover the pan with aluminum foil and bake for 25 to 30 minutes. Remove from the oven, uncover the pan, and let stand for 5 minutes before serving.

PREP TIME: 10 minutes
COOK TIME: 25 to 30 minutes
TOTAL TIME: 35 to 40 minutes

SMOKED GOUDA SALMON MUFFINS

A favorite snack around my home are English muffins topped with whatever makes sense at that moment. When we're feeling "fancy" we like to go the way of seafood and, of course, cheese! These quick, easy English muffins make for a great snack on the go or a treat when you just want to hang out and enjoy some good food.

2 Trader Joe's Classic English Muffins

4 teaspoons Trader Joe's Cream Cheese

¼ cup grated smoked Gouda

1 (4-ounce) package Trader Joe's Everything but the Bagel Seasoned Smoked Salmon

1. Preheat the oven to 375°F, then line a baking sheet with parchment paper. Split the English muffins and place all four pieces on the baking sheet.

2. Smear 1 teaspoon of cream cheese on each muffin piece, then sprinkle half of the Gouda over two of the pieces and layer half of the salmon on top. Sprinkle on the rest of the cheese and top with the other muffin halves.

3. Bake for 5 to 7 minutes, or until the cheese is melted. Remove from the oven and serve immediately.

PREP TIME: 3 to 5 minutes
COOK TIME: 5 to 7 minutes
TOTAL TIME: 8 to 12 minutes

Poultry Dishes for Two

- QUICK CILANTRO-GRAPE CHICKEN SALAD
- THE LAZY LAZY
- SPICY HONEY CHICKEN POTATO BAKE
- EASY CHICKEN ENCHILADA PIE
- CHICKEN-TOPPED CHAYOTE SQUASH
- CHICKEN AND HUMMUS-STUFFED PEPPERS
- TEX-MEX LOADED CHICKEN JICAMA FRIES
- CHICKEN SAUSAGE FRIED RICE
- TURKEY BACON CHEDDAR POCKETS

QUICK CILANTRO-GRAPE CHICKEN SALAD

You can use this chicken salad as a stand-alone quick lunch, on a sandwich, as a side dish, or divvied up as quick protein snacks. I do all of these, depending on the mood and need, and thoroughly enjoy this salad even several times a week.

2 Trader Joe's Organic Free Range Boneless Skinless Chicken Breasts, cooked and shredded

¼ cup Trader Joe's Organic Poppy Seed Dressing, or as needed

¼ cup Trader Joe's Unsalted Dry Toasted Pecan Pieces

1 handful fresh cilantro, stems removed and chopped

1 cup halved seedless red grapes

1 tablespoon cooked bacon bits (optional)

1. In a medium bowl, use a fork to combine the chicken and salad dressing. Next add in the pecans, chopped cilantro, grape halves, and bacon bits (if using). Stir together using a wooden spoon.

2. If the salad seems a little dry, add more dressing a tablespoon at a time until the salad is fully coated.

PREP TIME: 5 to 7 minutes

THE LAZY LAZY

Inspired by shepherd's pie, this dinner is a super easy, incredibly scrumptious meal—largely thanks to the Everything Bagel seasoning blend from TJ's. This is the laziest form of shepherd's pie I could make, after already dumbing down the steps previously. Thus, the Lazy Lazy was born.

2 medium or large sweet potatoes

water for boiling

1 cup Trader Joe's frozen Organic Peas

½ pound Trader Joe's Ground Beef 80% Lean 20% Fat

1 tablespoon Trader Joe's Everything but the Bagel Sesame Seasoning Blend

¾ teaspoon garlic powder

¾ teaspoon smoked paprika

½ teaspoon ground mustard

½ teaspoon chili powder

½ cup shredded cheddar cheese

1. Place the sweet potatoes in a medium saucepot, then add enough water to cover them by an inch or more. Set on the stovetop over medium-high heat and boil for 15 minutes. Then check to make sure the water is still covering them, add more if needed, and set the timer for another 15 minutes.

2. While the sweet potatoes are cooking for the second round, pour the peas into a small saucepan and add water to cover them by 2 or 3 inches. Turn the heat to medium and let cook until the meat is ready (see below).

3. Place the ground beef in a large skillet over medium heat. Break up the meat with a wooden spoon, stirring regularly until brown for about 7 minutes, then remove from the heat. Now turn off the heat under the peas and remove them from the stovetop. Drain and combine the peas with the ground beef in a heat-resistant bowl along with all the seasonings. Mix thoroughly to coat the pea-and-meat mixture, then set aside.

4. When the sweet potatoes have finished their second round, they should be tender and easy to smoosh with a fork. Turn off the heat and remove the pot from the burner. Using tongs, lift the potatoes onto two dinner plates. Use a fork and knife to open and spread them out somewhat on the plates. Sprinkle half the cheese on each sweet potato and smash it in with a fork. Then spoon half the meat mixture onto each potato.

ACTIVE TIME: 10 minutes
COOKING TIME: 30 minutes
TOTAL TIME: 40 minutes

SPICY HONEY CHICKEN POTATO BAKE

For a magical meal that's super easy to make, try this spicy honey chicken bake. Just a handful of simple ingredients turns into a delicious meal in less than an hour, with only 10 minutes of prep time.

½ (28-ounce) package Trader Joe's Mashed Potatoes, thawed

¼ cup Trader Joe's Organic Spicy Honey Sauce, divided

½ (8-ounce) package Trader Joe's Grilled Chicken Strips, thawed

3 green onions, chopped

1 handful fresh cilantro, chopped

1. Preheat the oven to 375°F. Lightly grease a loaf pan, then spread the mashed potatoes across the pan. Drizzle about half of the honey sauce over the potatoes.

2. Layer on the chicken strips, then sprinkle on the green onions and cilantro. Drizzle the remainder of the honey sauce over the dish and place it in the oven.

3. Bake for 15 to 20 minutes, then remove and let stand for 3 minutes before serving.

PREP TIME: 7 to 10 minutes
COOK TIME: 15 to 20 minutes
TOTAL TIME: 22 to 30 minutes

EASY CHICKEN ENCHILADA PIE

Growing up, I ate a lot of enchiladas with my family. My dad felt he had to make everything from scratch, including the enchilada sauce. As an adult, I love the idea of enchiladas, but until discovering Trader Joe's Enchilada Sauce I wasn't about to invest that much time into making them. Now I use the sauce for anything I can, including this twist on a chicken pot pie.

1 package Trader Joe's Pie Crusts, thawed

8 to 10 strips Trader Joe's frozen Grilled Chicken Strips, thawed

⅔ yellow or white onion, diced fine

1 red, yellow, or orange bell pepper, diced fine

2 Roma tomatoes, finely diced

¼ cup sour cream, or more for serving

2 tablespoons milk of choice

¼ cup Trader Joe's Enchilada Sauce, divided, or more for serving

¼ cup Trader Joe's Vegan Caramelized Onion Dip, or more for serving

1 teaspoon Trader Joe's Chile Lime Seasoning Blend

1. Preheat the oven to 400°F. Line a deep-dish pie pan with one of the pie crusts. Set the second crust aside.

2. In a medium bowl, combine the chicken strips, diced onion, diced pepper, and diced tomatoes with a wooden spoon. Mix together and then add the ¼ cup sour cream, milk, half the enchilada sauce, the onion dip, and the seasoning blend. Mix thoroughly until the chicken and veggies are well coated. Spoon the filling into the pie crust, then drizzle the remaining enchilada sauce over the top.

3. Top the pie with the second crust and seal the edges together, using your fingers or a fork; trim off the excess crust and cut slits in the top crust. Bake on the lower rack of the oven for 45 minutes, or until the crust is golden brown. Remove from the oven and let stand 5 minutes, then serve with additional enchilada sauce, sour cream, or caramelized onion dip, to taste.

PREP TIME: 10 minutes
COOK TIME: 45 minutes
TOTAL TIME: 55 minutes

CHICKEN-TOPPED CHAYOTE SQUASH

I'm always game for trying less-common veggies and fruits, so when I came across a squash that looked like a pear, I thought, why not? I read up on it and discovered that a chayote would taste a bit like a cross between a cucumber and a typical gourd. Immediately a shredded chicken-citrus topping came to mind. I was not disappointed.

2 chayote squash

2 green onions, chopped

1 cup cooked, shredded chicken breast

4 to 6 Trader Joe's Les Petites Carrots of Many Colors, peeled, cooked, and mashed

⅔ cup shredded cheddar cheese

1 teaspoon Trader Joe's Cuban Style Citrusy Garlic Seasoning Blend

½ teaspoon lime juice

1. Preheat the oven to 375°F. Place the chayote squash in a small, oven-safe baking dish, adding about 1 inch of water. Bake for 20 minutes, then remove from the oven and let cool for 15 minutes.

2. While the squash is cooling, combine the remaining ingredients in a medium bowl. Set aside.

3. Cut the cooled squash in half lengthwise. Trim off the ends and use a spoon to scoop out the seeds in the middle. Then arrange the squash on two plates and top with the carrot-chicken mixture.

4. Empty the baking pan of any remaining water and lightly spray it with olive oil spray. Return the squash to the pan, with the toppings, and bake for 10 more minutes, or until the cheese melts. Remove from the oven and let stand 3 minutes, then serve.

ACTIVE TIME: 10 minutes
COOKING TIME: 30 minutes
STANDING TIME: 18 minutes
TOTAL TIME: 48 minutes

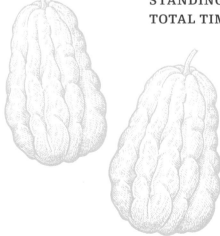

CHICKEN AND HUMMUS-STUFFED PEPPERS

Bell peppers, no matter the color, are my absolute favorite vegetable. I love the crisp texture of the raw veggie and the tenderness of a grilled bell pepper. I'll eat them plain for a snack or dipped in hummus for a protein kick. Even better is a stuffed and baked pepper—and this recipe combines these concepts for an easy, delicious meal. Serve it with a side of stuffed mushrooms, chicken salad, or garden salad for the perfect full meal.

2 red, yellow, or orange bell peppers, halved and seeded

1 Trader Joe's Organic Free Range Chicken Boneless Skinless Breast, cooked and shredded

½ cup Trader Joe's Organic Hummus

2 green onions, chopped

½ cup shredded mozzarella cheese

½ tablespoon milk of choice

1 teaspoon Trader Joe's Cuban Style Citrusy Garlic Seasoning Blend

4 dollops of sour cream, for garnish (optional)

1. Preheat the oven to 400°F, then line a baking sheet with parchment paper. Place the pepper halves on the baking sheet, side by side but not touching, and set aside.

2. In a medium bowl, combine all the remaining ingredients except the sour cream, working them together with a fork. Spoon a quarter of the mixture into each pepper half.

3. Place in the oven and bake for 7 minutes. Then remove and garnish each pepper half with a dollop of sour cream, if desired. Serve immediately.

PREP TIME: 6 to 7 minutes
COOK TIME: 7 minutes
TOTAL TIME: 13 to 14 minutes

TEX-MEX LOADED CHICKEN JICAMA FRIES

I fell in love with Tex-Mex loaded fries right around the time my husband and I got married. You see, there was this taco shop around the corner, and it offered the cheapest eats around for our struggling budget. Now I love to make these for date nights as a romantic throwback to our early marriage days, and especially for Valentine's Day—the first night we tried them.

1 (9.5-ounce) package Trader Joe's Jicama Sticks

1 tablespoon olive oil

1 cup Trader Joe's Fancy Shredded Mexican Style Cheese Blend, divided

1 teaspoon Trader Joe's Chile Lime Seasoning Blend

8 to 10 strips Trader Joe's Grilled Chicken Strips, thawed and cubed

2 Roma tomatoes, diced

1 red bell pepper, diced

½ jalapeño pepper, diced (optional)

1½ tablespoons Trader Joe's Enchilada Sauce

1. Preheat the oven to 400°F and line a baking sheet with parchment paper. Set the baking sheet on your work surface and spread the jicama sticks over it, side by side but not overlapping. Lightly drizzle the olive oil over the sticks.

2. Sprinkle on about half the cheese, followed by the seasoning blend. Then layer on the chicken, tomatoes, bell pepper, and jalapeño, spreading the ingredients out across the jicama sticks as evenly as possible.

3. Place in the oven and bake for 30 minutes, then sprinkle on the remaining ½ cup cheese and drizzle the enchilada sauce over the fries. Bake for 7 to 10 minutes longer, or until the fries are crisp. Remove from the oven and let stand for 3 minutes before serving.

PREP TIME: 10 minutes
COOK TIME: 37 to 40 minutes
TOTAL TIME: 47 to 50 minutes

CHICKEN SAUSAGE FRIED RICE

For a quick, easy dinner, whip up this sausage fried rice that offers a sweet, tangy flavor you'll want to gobble down. It's one of the quickest recipes in this book and tastes amazing, thanks to Trader Joe's premade fried rice.

1 tablespoon vegetable oil

2 links Trader Joe's Organic Sweet Italian Chicken Sausage, sliced into ½-inch slices

½ (8-ounce) package Trader Joe's Vegetable Fried Rice, thawed

¼ cup Trader Joe's 100% Pineapple Juice

1. Add the 1 tablespoon vegetable oil to a large skillet over medium heat. Add the sausage pieces and let cook for 3 minutes. Then use tongs to flip the pieces and cook for another 1 to 2 minutes.

2. Add the fried rice and pineapple juice to the pan. Stir constantly while the ingredients cook for 5 to 7 minutes, or until the pineapple juice disappears. Remove from the heat and serve immediately.

PREP TIME: 2 minutes
COOK TIME: 9 to 12 minutes
TOTAL TIME: 11 to 14 minutes

TURKEY BACON CHEDDAR POCKETS

I love quick, easy snacks that can double as meals, like these Turkey Bacon Cheddar Pockets. They're great for nights when you're not sure how hungry you are, or you just want something to accompany that healthy side salad.

1 (8-ounce) container Trader Joe's Crescent Rolls

2 to 3 tablespoons olive oil

2 egg whites, whisked

1 tablespoon Trader Joe's Everything but the Bagel Sesame Seasoning Blend

6 to 8 strips uncooked Trader Joe's Uncured Turkey Bacon, cut into bite-sized pieces

½ to ¾ cup shredded or chunked Trader Joe's English Cheddar with Caramelized Onions or Trader Joe's New Zealand Sharp Cheddar Cheese

1. Preheat the oven to 375°F and line a baking sheet with parchment paper. Sprinkle your work surface with flour and unpackage the crescent dough onto the prepared surface. Divide it into the premade sections, then lightly brush olive oil over the dough.

2. Sprinkle the seasoning blend evenly across the dough pieces. Place pieces of turkey bacon onto each dough piece along with a chunk or large pinch of the cheddar cheese.

3. Wrap the dough around the meat and cheese and press the edges together to create pockets. Leave one small opening on each pocket, then prick each pocket with a fork a few times. Brush egg white over each pocket, then place on the baking sheet and pop it into the oven.

4. Bake for 17 to 20 minutes, or until lightly browned. Remove from the oven and quickly transfer the pockets to a plate or platter. Let rest for 5 to 7 minutes before serving.

PREP TIME: 12 to 15 minutes
COOK TIME: 17 to 20 minutes
TOTAL TIME: 29 to 35 minutes

Salads and Soups

- ROASTED RED PEPPER TOMATO WILD RICE SOUP
- GLUTEN-FREE TOMATO ENDIVE PASTA SOUP
- BLACK FOREST BACON AND CHICKEN SALAD
- ROASTED RED PEPPER TOMATO BEAN SOUP
- PEPPERCORN PORK SALAD
- CRUCIFEROUS CRUNCH SAUSAGE SALAD
- SWEET APPLE CHICKEN SALAD WITH HONEY CITRUS DRESSING
- BBQ PIZZA SALAD WITH HOMEMADE CROUTONS
- SEAFOOD FRUIT SALAD
- CITRUSY GARLIC PLANTAIN CHICKEN SALAD

ROASTED RED PEPPER TOMATO WILD RICE SOUP

My family was never huge into tomato soup when I was growing up, but I remember discovering as a teenager the immense comfort a bowl could provide. Since that time, I have frequently enjoyed a nice, warm bowl of tomato soup, and now I like to share a hearty bowl with my hubby on cool evenings. I use Trader Joe's Organic Tomato & Roasted Red Pepper Soup as a solid foundation, and this new favorite version also includes wild rice and cheese.

2 cups Trader Joe's
Organic Tomato & Roasted
Red Pepper Soup

1 cup cooked wild rice

¼ cup sour cream

½ cup shredded
mozzarella cheese

2 green onions, chopped

1. Pour the soup into a medium saucepan and set it over medium-low heat. Stir occasionally. After about 5 minutes, when the soup has heated up, add the cooked wild rice (reserve some cooked rice for garnishing), sour cream, cheese, and green onions, stirring constantly to prevent the cheese from burning. Keep stirring until the cheese is melted and blended in, about 4 minutes.

2. Remove the pan from the heat. Then ladle the soup into two bowls. Top with extra cooked rice and enjoy while it's still steaming.

PREP TIME: 4 minutes
COOKING TIME: 9 minutes

GLUTEN-FREE TOMATO ENDIVE PASTA SOUP

I adore tomato soup. My husband, not so much. So I've had to get creative about how to serve up a bowl of warm something. One of the best bases for this project is the roasted red-pepper tomato soup at Trader Joe's. I add all kinds of tasty things to make it even heartier—in this case, endives, pasta, and cheese.

Trader Joe's Organic Brown Rice & Quinoa Fussili Pasta to make 1 cup

2 cups Trader Joe's Organic Tomato & Roasted Red Pepper Soup

1 package (3 heads) Trader Joe's Belgian Endives

½ cup shredded mozzarella cheese, plus more for topping if desired

½ cup sour cream

1. Following the package directions, cook enough of the pasta to yield 1 cup. Then strain and set aside.

2. While the pasta cooks, pour the 2 cups of soup into a medium saucepan and set over medium-low heat. Stir occasionally. While the soup warms, chop the endives into bite-size pieces.

3. When the soup has heated for about 5 minutes, add the chopped endives, cooked pasta, and ⅓ cup shredded cheese. Continually stir until the cheese melts and blends in. Then remove the soup from the stovetop and let it rest for 2 minutes.

4. Ladle the soup into two bowls and top with the sour cream. Sprinkle a little additional cheese on top, if desired.

ACTIVE TIME: 7 minutes
COOKING TIME: 10 minutes
TOTAL TIME: 17 minutes

BLACK FOREST BACON AND CHICKEN SALAD

We're big on salads in our household—but they can get boring if you use the same ingredients over and over, so experimentation is frequently called for. That's where this bacon, chicken, and fruit salad came from. I love using fresh fruit in salads with chicken, but the right cheese and a hint of bacon can make a huge difference, too.

4 strips Trader Joe's Uncured Black Forest Bacon

1½ tablespoons olive or grapeseed oil

1 large boneless, skinless chicken breast, diced into large cubes

bread crumbs for breading (optional)

6 cups spring mix lettuce

¼ cup Trader Joe's Crumbled Goat Cheese

½ cup fresh blueberries

½ cup halved and pitted cherries

½ cup fresh raspberries

½ cup fresh green grapes, sliced

4 tablespoons Trader Joe's Chunky Blue Cheese Dressing & Dip

1. Preheat the oven to 400°F. Line a baking sheet with parchment paper, then lay out the bacon pieces, side by side, on the sheet. Cook for 12 to 20 minutes (12 minutes will cook the bacon, but 20 will make it crisp in most cases).

2. While the bacon is cooking, lightly oil a large skillet with the olive or grapeseed oil. Turn the heat on to medium-low and warm the oil for about 3 minutes, then add the diced chicken and cook undisturbed for 4 minutes. Then flip the chicken pieces—I use tongs for less oil splash! Optional: you can also coat the chicken in bread crumbs. Cook for another 3 to 4 minutes, or until the chicken is slightly singed and brown. Make sure the meat is cooked all the way through before removing it from the heat, then set aside.

3. When the bacon is cooked, remove it from the oven and use tongs to transfer it to a paper towel–lined plate to drain.

4. Set out two dinner plates, divide the lettuce between them, and sprinkle half the crumbled goat cheese on each lettuce pile. Next add the cooked chicken, then the blueberries, cherries, raspberries, and green grapes. Crumble the bacon and sprinkle it on the salads. Top with the salad dressing and serve immediately.

PREP TIME: 7 minutes
COOK TIME: 22 to 31 minutes
TOTAL TIME: 29 to 38 minutes

ROASTED RED PEPPER TOMATO BEAN SOUP

I'm a huge fan of soup, but I need more in my soup than just liquid. With Trader Joe's Organic Tomato & Roasted Red Pepper Soup, a few veggie ingredients take it to the next level—especially with some cheese added to top it off.

2 cups Trader Joe's Organic Tomato & Roasted Red Pepper Soup

2 green onions, chopped

1 cup Trader Joe's Organic Black Beans, rinsed and drained

1 cup chopped baby spinach

⅔ cup shredded cheddar cheese

1. Pour the soup into a medium saucepan and turn the heat to medium-low. Add the onions, beans, and spinach, stirring to combine thoroughly.

2. Once the soup has warmed, after about 5 minutes, add the shredded cheese. Stir continuously until the cheese melts, then ladle the soup into two bowls and serve immediately.

PREP TIME: 5 minutes
COOKING TIME: 5 minutes
TOTAL TIME: 10 minutes

PEPPERCORN PORK SALAD

One thing I particularly love about TJ's seasoned meats is that they're flavored so well. All I have to do is plop them in the slow cooker or toss them in the oven and let them cook. In this case, I opted for the delicious peppercorn-garlic pork tenderloin as the meat topping for a salad. Toss in sun-dried tomatoes and fire roasted peppers, and it's a feast!

8 ounces Trader Joe's Peppercorn-Garlic Boneless Pork Tenderloin

olive oil spray

1 (7-ounce) package Trader Joe's Baby Wild Arugula

2 Trader Joe's Fire Roasted Red Peppers, chopped

¼ cup Trader Joe's Julienne Sliced Sun Dried Tomatoes

½ cup shredded Swiss cheese

4 tablespoons (¼ cup) Trader Joe's Balsamic Vinaigrette or Trader Joe's Vegan Creamy Dill Dressing

1. Using kitchen shears, cut the pork tenderloin into ½-inch medallions. Add a fine mist of olive oil to both sides of the medallions, then lay them in a skillet. Cook for 5 minutes, then flip and cook for another 5 minutes. Test with a thermometer—the internal temperature should reach 145°F. If the pork needs to cook longer, continue flipping the medallions over every 2 minutes to avoid burning them.

2. When the pork is ready, remove it from the heat and let it rest. Divide the arugula between two dinner plates, then top it with the red peppers and sun-dried tomatoes.

3. Sprinkle the shredded Swiss cheese onto the salads, then arrange the meat pieces on top of the cheese. Drizzle on the dressing and serve immediately.

PREP TIME: 7 to 10 minutes
COOK TIME: 10 minutes
TOTAL TIME: 17 to 20 minutes

CRUCIFEROUS CRUNCH SAUSAGE SALAD

Not all salads require lettuce, tomatoes, and ranch dressing. In fact, I much prefer the twist of ingredients that aren't "supposed" to be in salads. This flavorful salad mixture really gets me excited—it's so delicious!

1 (12-ounce) package (5 links) Trader Joe's Roasted Garlic Chicken Sausage

4 cups (roughly 1½ packages) Trader Joe's Cruciferous Crunch Collection

4 tablespoons (¼ cup) Trader Joe's Vegan Caesar Dressing, or more as desired

1 ounce Trader Joe's Organic Crumbled Feta Cheese

½ cup crushed Trader Joe's Roasted Plantain Chips (optional)

1. Preheat the oven to 375°F. Place the sausages on a vented baking pan, then prick a few holes into each sausage. Set the pan in the oven and cook the sausages for 10 minutes.

2. While the sausages are heating, in a large skillet over medium heat lightly sauté the cruciferous crunch mixture in the salad dressing for about 4 minutes. Remove from the heat and let stand, and remove the sausages from the oven.

3. When everything has cooled for 3 minutes, cut the sausages into 1½-inch chunks and in a large bowl, toss them with the cruciferous medley and the feta cheese. Divide the mixture between two plates, drizzling with more dressing if desired. Serve immediately, with the crushed plantain chips sprinkled over the salads.

ACTIVE TIME: 9 minutes
COOKING TIME: 14 minutes
STANDING TIME: 3 minutes
TOTAL TIME: 26 minutes

SWEET APPLE CHICKEN SALAD WITH HONEY CITRUS DRESSING

Another quick, easy, and oh-so-good salad is this apple-chicken combo with a sweet homemade dressing. It's perfect for a low-key evening when you just want some extra brightness or for a summer date on the patio for the two of you.

FOR THE SALAD DRESSING:

½ teaspoon Trader Joe's Hawaiian Macadamia Nut Blossom & Multi-Floral Honey

1 teaspoon apple cider vinegar

2 tablespoons Trader Joe's Organic Cold Pressed Orange Juice

½ teaspoon lemon juice

1 teaspoon grapeseed oil

½ teaspoon Trader Joe's Cuban Style Citrusy Garlic Seasoning Blend

FOR THE SALAD:

8 to 10 strips Trader Joe's Grilled Chicken Strips, thawed

6 cups baby kale

½ cup shredded cheddar cheese

2 apples (Fuji, Pink Lady, Yellow Delicious, or Gala), seeded and chopped into bite-size pieces

2 tablespoons walnut or pecan pieces

pomegranate seeds

blue cheese bits (optional)

1. In an airtight jar or salad dressing shaker, combine all the ingredients for the salad dressing. Seal and shake thoroughly, then set aside.

2. Warm the chicken strips in the microwave for about 1 minute on high. While the chicken is warming, set out two dinner plates and divide the kale between them. Then add the warmed chicken and immediately top with the cheese, allowing it to melt slightly. Finish the salads with the apples, nuts, seeds, and cheese bits, if desired.

3. Drizzle half the dressing on each plate and serve immediately.

PREP TIME: 15 minutes

BBQ PIZZA SALAD WITH HOMEMADE CROUTONS

Three of my favorite types of food are barbecue, pizza, and salad. So, I thought, why not combine them into one delicious meal? Enjoy!

¼ Trader Joe's Pizza Crust (prebaked)

1 tablespoon olive oil

4 cups Trader Joe's Organic Baby Spinach

32 slices turkey pepperoni

½ cup Trader Joe's Shredded Pizza Seasoned Toscano Cheese

4 tablespoons Trader Joe's Organic Kansas City Style BBQ Sauce

1. Preheat the oven to 375°F. Line a baking sheet with parchment paper and set aside. On your work surface, lightly brush the pizza crust with olive oil, then flip and brush the other side. Cut the crust into crouton-size pieces. Using tongs, arrange the crust cubes in a single layer on the baking sheet so they're not touching each other. Bake for 10 minutes, then use tongs to flip the croutons over and bake for another 5 to 7 minutes, until golden brown. Remove from the oven and transfer the crust cubes to a tea towel to cool completely, for about an hour.

2. When the croutons have cooled, set out two dinner plates. First layer on the spinach, half per plate, then top with the pepperoni slices. Sprinkle the cheese evenly across the plates, drizzle the BBQ sauce over the salads, and top with the toasted croutons. Serve immediately.

PREP TIME: 7 to 10 minutes
COOK TIME: 15 to 17 minutes
REST TIME: 1 hour
TOTAL TIME: 1 hour 12 minutes to 1 hour 27 minutes

SEAFOOD FRUIT SALAD

This recipe is a longtime family favorite. We stumbled across the basic idea back in the early 2000s, and over the years it has morphed into this now-standard form. It's one of our favorite date-night meals.

2 strips Trader Joe's Uncured Apple Smoked Bacon

1 red-skinned apple, diced

1 green-skinned apple, diced

1 orange or 2 clementines, peeled and diced

1 cup halved seedless green grapes

1 cup halved seedless red grapes

1 banana, thinly sliced

2 green onions, chopped

4 ounces flake-style imitation crab meat, chunked

½ pound shrimp of choice, cooked and peeled, with tails removed

6 tablespoons Trader Joe's Organic Poppy Seed Dressing or Trader Joe's Buttermilk Ranch Dressing, or more as needed

1. Preheat the oven to 400°F. Line a baking sheet with parchment paper, then lay the bacon out, side by side, on the sheet. Cook for 12 to 20 minutes, to desired crispness.

2. While the bacon is cooking, combine everything else except the salad dressing in a large mixing bowl. Use a wooden spoon to mix together until everything is well integrated. Then add the salad dressing and mix again to coat everything with the dressing. If needed, add 1 more tablespoon of dressing at a time and remix until everything is coated properly. Cover the bowl and put in the fridge to chill for 1 to 2 hours.

3. When the bacon is crisp, remove it from the oven and use tongs to place it on a paper towel–lined plate to drain. Let the bacon drain for about 15 minutes, then put it in a container with more clean paper towels and place in the fridge along with the salad. Once the salad and bacon have chilled, divide the salad between two plates, crumble the bacon on top, and enjoy.

PREP TIME: 15 minutes
COOK TIME: 12 to 20 minutes
TOTAL TIME: 22 to 30 minutes

CITRUSY GARLIC PLANTAIN CHICKEN SALAD

Quick and easy to prepare, this is one of the tastiest, tangiest, and sweetest salads around. Serve it for a casual night together, a quick lunch, or a relaxed evening meal on the patio in the summer.

4 tablespoons Trader Joe's Buttermilk Ranch Dressing

1 teaspoon Trader Joe's Cuban Style Citrusy Garlic Seasoning Blend

6 cups Trader Joe's Baby Wild Arugula (about 1½ bags)

½ package Trader Joe's Plantain Crisps

8 to 10 strips Trader Joe's Grilled Chicken Strips, thawed

1 fresh mango, peeled and diced

1. In a small bowl, combine the salad dressing and seasoning blend and mix until thoroughly combined. Set aside.

2. Set out two dinner plates and place half the arugula on each plate. Layer on the plantain chips, half per plate, and then the chicken strips and mango. Drizzle the dressing over the salad and serve immediately.

PREP TIME: 5 to 6 minutes

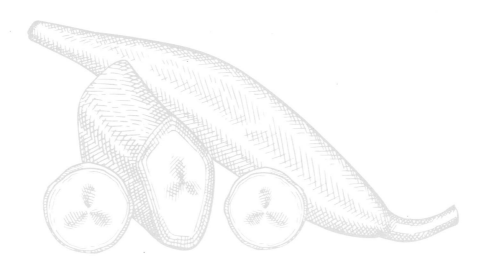

Meaty Mains for Two

- FIG BUTTER-GLAZED PORK CHOPS
- BAKED ALFREDO HAM
- SAUSAGE-TOPPED SWEET POTATOES
- GLUTEN-FREE CAULIFLOWER SAUSAGE SHEPHERD'S PIE
- EASY ITALIAN SAUSAGE KABOBS
- HAM AND ALFREDO MASH
- CITRUS GARLIC-BUTTER RIB EYE
- SWEET AND SPICY SAUSAGE SKEWERS
- LEMON-CHERRY BEEF FLANK STEAK

FIG BUTTER-GLAZED PORK CHOPS

For an easy, tasty, and unique dinner for two, try these flavorful pork chops inspired by Trader Joe's terrific Fig Butter. Pork is best with fruit (in my opinion!), so with a tangy, sweet fruit glaze it's just about perfect.

¼ cup Trader Joe's Fig Butter

2 teaspoons apple juice

1 tablespoon balsamic vinegar

1 teaspoon coconut oil, melted

1 tablespoon unsalted butter, melted

1 teaspoon dried thyme

2 Trader Joe's Boneless Center Cut Pork Loin Chops

1. Preheat the oven to 400°F. Lightly oil a grill pan and place it on the stovetop over medium-high heat to warm for 5 minutes. While the pan is heating, combine the fig butter, apple juice, vinegar, coconut oil, butter, and thyme in a small bowl and mix until the ingredients are thoroughly incorporated as a glaze.

2. Place the pork chops in the stovetop heated pan and brush with about a third of the glaze. Immediately flip and cook for 5 minutes. Then baste the chops with another third of the glaze, flip again, and cook for another 5 minutes. Baste the chops with the remainder of the glaze and bake in the oven for 10 to 12 more minutes, or until the internal temperature of the chops reaches 145°F. Remove from the oven, let rest for 3 minutes, and then serve.

PREP TIME: 3 to 5 minutes
COOK TIME: 25 to 27 minutes
TOTAL TIME: 28 to 32 minutes

BAKED ALFREDO HAM

We know that ham and cheese go well as sandwich fillers—the ultimate classic easy lunch. So why not a cheesy stuffed ham with a unique Italian-inspired flair? This moderately easy meal is rich and delicious, perfect for a low-key date night.

¼ cup Trader Joe's Organic Bread Crumbs

1 tablespoon milk of choice

1 cup Trader Joe's Limone Alfredo Sauce, divided

2 green onions, chopped

½ cup shredded Trader Joe's New Zealand Sharp Cheddar Cheese

1 Trader Joe's Fire Roasted Red Pepper, chopped

1-pound block cooked ham

½ cup apple juice

1 tablespoon olive oil

1 tablespoon lemon juice

1 teaspoon Italian seasoning

1 teaspoon Trader Joe's Italian Style Soffritto Seasoning Blend

1. Preheat the oven to 400°F. In a medium bowl, combine the bread crumbs, milk, ½ cup alfredo sauce, green onions, cheese, and roasted red pepper. Mix with a wooden spoon until thoroughly combined, then set aside.

2. Place the block of ham on your work surface and, working out from the center, cut a slit ⅔ of the way across and into the meat, leaving the ham intact on both ends of the slit. Rotate the ham and repeat the action, creating a cut shaped like a plus sign. Use a fork to spread the cut out; if needed, cut away chunks of meat to enlarge the cavity slightly. Stuff the cavity with about half of the filling, cutting away more ham as you go if necessary bit leaving the edges intact. Set the stuffed ham in a lightly greased 9 x 9-inch baking dish with a lid. Cover and set aside.

3. In a small jar, combine the apple juice, olive oil, lemon juice, Italian seasoning, and soffritto seasoning blend. Cover and shake vigorously, then pour the mixture into the pan with the ham. Place all the remaining stuffing in the pan with the ham, then cover the pan with aluminum foil.

4. Bake the ham for 40 minutes, then uncover and bake for another 15 minutes. Remove from the oven, pour the remaining alfredo sauce over the ham, and let stand for 10 minutes. Cut the ham into slices and serve with the extra stuffing.

PREP TIME: 15 minutes
COOK TIME: 55 minutes
STAND TIME: 10 minutes
TOTAL TIME: 1 hour, 20 minutes

SAUSAGE-TOPPED SWEET POTATOES

While a lot of folks think of sweet potatoes as a side dish, this sausage-topped version is definitely a full meal. I usually can't even finish one serving on my own! Thankfully, though, my husband loves it—and standing at 6'5", he has a bigger appetite and enjoys my leftovers.

2 large sweet potatoes

½ tablespoon unsalted butter

½ cup shredded Trader Joe's Smoked Gouda

1 teaspoon Trader Joe's Cuban Style Citrusy Garlic Seasoning Blend

2 links Trader Joe's Sweet Italian Sausage Made with Pork, cooked and cut into bite-size pieces

1. Preheat the oven to 425°F and line a baking sheet with foil. Place the sweet potatoes on the foil and use a fork to prick several holes in each one. Place in the oven and bake for 40 to 50 minutes, or until they feel soft when pressed with a fork. Remove from the oven and let rest for 5 minutes.

2. When the sweet potatoes have started to cool, set them on plates and cut each one open down the middle. Use a fork to spread them out a bit. Place a pat of butter in each sweet potato, then sprinkle on the cheese and then the seasoning blend. Top with the sausage pieces and serve immediately.

PREP TIME: 7 minutes
COOK TIME: 40 to 50 minutes
TOTAL TIME: 47 to 57 minutes

GLUTEN-FREE CAULIFLOWER SAUSAGE SHEPHERD'S PIE

One of my absolute favorite hearty meals is a shepherd's pie. But I can get bored with the same old ingredients, so I like to mix things up. One of my new favorite alternatives is using mashed cauliflower instead of mashed potatoes as the topper and sausage pieces for the filling.

4 Trader Joe's Sweet Italian Sausage Made with Pork, cut into ½ to ¾-inch chunks

2 cups Trader Joe's Mirepoix Chopped Vegetable Mix

1 tablespoon all-purpose flour

1 tablespoon milk of choice

½ tablespoon Worcestershire sauce

½ (8-ounce) package Trader Joe's Mashed Cauliflower, thawed

1 teaspoon garlic powder

1 teaspoon dried parsley

1 teaspoon dried rosemary

¼ teaspoon salt

¼ teaspoon ground black pepper

1. Preheat the oven to 400°F, then lightly oil a cast-iron skillet and set it over medium-high heat to warm for about 3 minutes. Then add the sausage pieces and cook for 2 to 3 minutes. Using tongs, flip the pieces and cook for another 1 to 2 minutes, then remove from the heat.

2. In a medium bowl, combine the cooked sausage pieces, mirepoix vegetable mix, flour, milk, and Worcestershire sauce. Mix with a wooden spoon until the sausage and vegetables are coated, then set aside.

3. In a separate mixing bowl, combine the mashed cauliflower, garlic, parsley, rosemary, salt, and pepper, incorporating the seasonings well into the cauliflower mash.

4. Place the sausage and vegetables in the cast-iron skillet, spreading the mixture evenly across the pan. Then spread the seasoned cauliflower mash over the top. Bake, uncovered, for 20 to 25 minutes, or until the mash turns "crusty" and browns at the edges and in the middle. Remove from the oven and serve while hot.

PREP TIME: 7 to 10 minutes
COOK TIME: 20 to 25 minutes
TOTAL TIME: 27 to 35 minutes

EASY ITALIAN SAUSAGE KABOBS

Thanks to living in Germany for a couple of years, my parents instilled in me the love of German food—particularly sausages and brats. Now I love using these in all kinds of recipes, and I particularly appreciate them as seared skewer meat with veggies.

¼ cup olive oil

½ cup apple juice

1 teaspoon Trader Joe's Ajika Georgian Seasoning Blend

½ teaspoon onion powder

4 Trader Joe's Chicken Apple Chardonnay Sausages, cut into ¾-inch chunks

1 red bell pepper, cut into chunks

1 yellow bell pepper, cut into chunks

1 red onion, cut into chunks

1 zucchini, cut into chunks

**SPECIAL EQUIPMENT:
4 TO 6 SKEWERS**

1. Combine the olive oil, apple juice, seasoning blend, and onion powder in a 1-gallon ziplock bag or other watertight container. Add the sausage pieces, bell pepper chunks, zucchini, and red onion chunks, then seal the bag and shake it vigorously to coat everything. Squeeze the air out of the bag, seal tightly, and fold the bag over so the contents stay in contact with the marinade. Place in the refrigerator for 30 minutes.

2. Remove the bag from the fridge. Thread the sausage pieces and veggies onto 4 to 6 skewers, alternating ingredients until all are used and reserving the leftover marinade.

3. Lightly oil a cast-iron skillet and warm it over medium-high heat for 3 minutes. Then pour in the reserved marinade and set the skewers in the pan. Baste the skewers with the marinade and cook for 5 minutes. Then, using tongs, flip the skewers and baste the other side. Cook for 5 more minutes. Repeat as needed until the sausage pieces begin to look seared; this should take no more than two flips each. Remove from the heat and serve immediately.

PREP TIME: 10 minutes
COOK TIME: 13 to 18 minutes
REST TIME: 30 minutes
TOTAL TIME: 53 to 58 minutes

HAM AND ALFREDO MASH

I love dishes that you can mix together in one basic step and then toss in the oven. I also love mashed potatoes and cheese. For this flavorful meal, I mixed in some tasty Trader Joe's ingredients for a wholly unique mash bake, and I've loved every bite every time. The cheese curds make a nice, crunchy addition.

10 ounces cooked ham, diced

2 cups thawed Trader Joe's Mashed Potatoes

¼ cup Trader Joe's Julienne Sliced Sun-Dried Tomatoes

1½ teaspoons Trader Joe's Italian Style Soffritto Seasoning Blend

1 teaspoon garlic powder

¼ cup milk of choice

8 ounces (half package) Trader Joe's Breaded Cheddar Cheese Curds

½ cup Trader Joe's Limone Alfredo Sauce

1. Preheat the oven to 350°F. In a medium bowl, combine the ham, mashed potatoes, sun-dried tomatoes, seasoning blend, and garlic powder with a wooden spoon. Next add the milk and the Alfredo sauce and combine thoroughly.

2. Spread the mash into a lightly greased 9 x 5-inch loaf pan or 4 to 5 individual ramekins. Pop it into the oven and bake for 20 minutes, or until the mashed potatoes are golden brown on top.

3. Evenly spread the cheese curds over the dish, then bake for another 15 minutes.

4. Remove from the oven and let stand for 3 to 4 minutes before serving.

PREP TIME: 7 minutes
COOK TIME: 30 to 35 minutes
TOTAL TIME: 37 to 42 minutes

CITRUS GARLIC-BUTTER RIB EYE

If I'm going to eat steak, it's got to be really good. That means good seasoning, good sauce, and a good cut. In this case, taking a good ribeye cut and adding just a hint of tenderness via butter and that amazing flavor of a Trader Joe's seasoning blend is all it takes.

1 Trader Joe's Grass Fed Organic Rib Eye Beef Steak

1 tablespoon unsalted butter, softened

1 teaspoon Trader Joe's Cuban Style Citrusy Garlic Seasoning Blend

1. Warm a medium cast-iron skillet or grill pan on the stovetop over medium-high heat for about 7 minutes. As the pan heats, rinse off the steak and pat it dry with a paper towel, then set aside.

2. In a small bowl, use a fork to combine the butter and seasoning blend until the seasoning is incorporated throughout the butter.

3. When the pan is hot, add the steak. Cook for 5 minutes and then use tongs to flip the meat. Add half the seasoned butter to the top and cook for another 2 to 3 minutes, brushing the butter over the meat. Then flip again, brush the rest of the butter across the meat, and cook for another 1 or 2 minutes.

4. Transfer the steak to a plate and cover with aluminum foil. Let rest for 15 minutes, then remove the foil, slice the meat, and serve.

PREP TIME: 5 to 7 minutes
COOK TIME: 8 to 10 minutes
REST TIME: 15 minutes
TOTAL TIME: 28 to 32 minutes

SWEET AND SPICY SAUSAGE SKEWERS

Skewered sausages are a flavorful, fun meal at any time of the year. They pair perfectly with rice, potatoes, or a side of roasted veggies, and they take little effort to prepare. My husband and I thoroughly enjoy making these together as part of an at-home date night.

4 links Trader Joe's Sweet Italian Sausage Made with Pork

1 cup Trader Joe's 100% Pineapple Juice

1 teaspoon Trader Joe's Chile Lime Seasoning Blend

1 teaspoon garlic powder

2 firm, fresh peaches, sliced

2 red bell peppers, cut in large pieces

2 green bell peppers, cut in large pieces

1 red onion, cut in large pieces

SPECIAL EQUIPMENT: 3 SKEWERS

1. Preheat the oven to 400°F and line a baking sheet with parchment paper. Puncture the sausage links several times with a fork and place them on the baking sheet. Bake for 20 to 25 minutes, then remove from the oven and let cool for 15 minutes. Then cut the sausages into ½-inch slices and set aside.

2. Pour the pineapple juice into a watertight container or plastic ziplock bag. Add the lime seasoning and garlic powder, then seal and shake vigorously to blend. Next add the sausage, peach, bell pepper, and onion pieces to the marinade. Seal again, removing excess air if using a bag and folding it over to keep the ingredients awash in the marinade. Chill in the refrigerator for 3 hours to let the ingredients soak in the marinade.

3. When the ingredients have marinated, lightly oil a medium griddle or cast-iron skillet and set it on the stove over medium-high heat. Remove the package from the fridge and carefully skewer a mixture of the ingredients onto four skewers, alternating ingredients. Discard the marinade.

4. Place the skewers directly on the heated griddle or pan surface and cook for 3 minutes. Then use tongs to flip the skewers and cook for another 3 minutes. Remove from the heat and serve immediately.

PREP TIME: 15 minutes
COOK TIME: 26 to 31 minutes
REST TIME: 3 hours 15 minutes
TOTAL TIME: 3 hours 56 minutes to 4 hours 1 minute

LEMON-CHERRY BEEF FLANK STEAK

I'm admittedly not a huge fan of beef, but I've found a way that both the hubby and I can enjoy a good steak for a special treat. Adding fruit to almost anything seals it for me. For him, it's all about the beef. And though it might sound a little unusual, this lemon-cherry marinated beef has become that winner for us.

½ cup Trader Joe's Organic Cold Pressed Orange Juice

1 tablespoon olive oil

¼ cup lemon juice

15 ounces canned dark, sweet cherries in heavy syrup

1 tablespoon light brown sugar

2 green onions, finely chopped

1 teaspoon garlic powder

¼ teaspoon salt

1 pound (approximate) Trader Joe's USDA Choice Premium Angus Beef Flank Steak

1 tablespoon Trader Joe's Lemon Curd

1. Pour the orange juice into a ziplock bag or an airtight container with a lid, large enough to hold the flank steak. Next add the olive oil, lemon juice, cherries with syrup, brown sugar, green onions, garlic powder, and salt. Seal the container and shake vigorously to blend the marinade. Then place the steak in the container and reseal. If using a ziplock bag, be sure to squeeze the air out and fold the bag over to keep the meat covered in the marinade. Let the steak marinate in the refrigerator for 6 to 8 hours.

2. When the steak has marinated, lightly oil a medium or large cast-iron skillet and place it over medium heat. Warm the skillet for 5 minutes, then remove the steak from the marinade and place it in the skillet. Cook on one side for 4 minutes, then use tongs to flip the steak over and cook for another 4 minutes.

3. Reduce the heat to medium-low, pour in the marinade (including the cherries), and let the steak cook for 2 to 3 more minutes. Then use a spatula or butter knife to smear the lemon curd over the meat. Flip the steak and cook for another 2 to 3 minutes, or until your desired doneness is reached. Remove the steak from the pan, discard the marinade, and cut the meat into slices to serve.

PREP TIME: 5 minutes
REST TIME: 6 to 8 hours
COOK TIME: 17 to 9 minutes
TOTAL TIME: 6 hours 22 minutes to 8 hours 24 minutes

Desserts to Share

- CREAMY SPICED CHAI ICE MILK
- CARAMEL SPICED CHAI COCONUT POPSICLES
- CARROT LOAF FOR TWO
- MINI MOCHI PINEAPPLE UPSIDE-DOWN CAKE
- CHEVRE HONEY BLUEBERRY TARTLETS
- PEANUT BUTTER BALLS
- GLUTEN-FREE COCONUT MOCHI CAKE DONUTS
- HOMEMADE STRAWBERRY POMEGRANATE ICE CREAM
- PEPPERMINT HOT CHOCOLATE ICE CREAM SUNDAES
- ICED VEGAN CHIA PUDDING

CREAMY SPICED CHAI ICE MILK

I'm a huge fan of all things Indian, having grown up eating Indian food in my grandmother's kitchen. She got her recipes from the source: friends who had immigrated to the U.S. from India in the 1970s. When I spotted the Spiced Chai Concentrate on Trader Joe's shelves, I knew I'd have to find some delectable goodies to make with it. This simple ice milk dessert is a new favorite.

1 tablespoon Trader Joe's Blanched Almond Flour

1 tablespoon tapioca or corn starch

1 cup sweetened vanilla almond milk

1 cup 1% dairy milk

1 cup Trader Joe's Spiced Chai Black Tea Concentrate

1 teaspoon vanilla extract

2 tablespoon walnut, almond, or pecan pieces (optional)

whipped cream (optional), for serving

toppings of choice, such as pecans or sprinkles

1. In a small saucepan, whisk together the almond flour and tapioca or corn starch. Pour in both milks and the chai tea concentrate, then whisk together until thoroughly combined. Set on the stovetop over medium-low and slowly bring to a light boil, not stirring. When the milk froths suddenly, quickly turn off the heat. Gently whisk in the vanilla extract. When combined, remove from the stove and mix in the nuts, if using.

2. Let cool for 10 minutes, then pour into a freezer-safe container with a lid. Seal and freeze for 6 hours or overnight. To serve, scoop into bowls, top with whipped cream as desired, and sprinkle with pecans, colored sprinkles, or other toppings of choice.

CARAMEL SPICED CHAI COCONUT POPSICLES

Who doesn't love a popsicle? Even better is a spicy, sweet, caramel chai popsicle! For this recipe, I use some of my absolute favorite flavors of all time to create the perfect creamy summer (or anytime) treat.

¼ Trader Joe's Spiced Chai Black Tea Concentrate

½ cup Trader Joe's Organic Coconut Milk

4 to 6 drops caramel flavoring

SPECIAL EQUIPMENT: POPSICLE MOLDS

1. In a small saucepan, combine the spiced chai concentrate and coconut milk over medium-low heat. Using a whisk, blend the two liquids together for 4 to 5 minutes, or until simmering. Turn off the heat and let stand for 2 to 3 minutes, then add the caramel flavoring, stirring to combine. Let cool for another 10 minutes, then pour into popsicle molds. Freeze for 6 to 8 hours and then enjoy!

COOK TIME: 4 to 5 minutes
PREP TIME: 5 minutes
REST TIME: 6 to 8 hours
TOTAL TIME: 6 hours 9 minutes to 8 hours 10 minutes

•••

Tip: To add some texture and extra flavor to your pops, stir in 1 tablespoon each of shredded coconut and pecan pieces right after you turn off the heat.

•••

CARROT LOAF FOR TWO

A sweetly spicy dessert is the perfect way to enjoy an evening together— especially when there's buttercream frosting involved! This little loaf for two (admittedly, you may have leftovers) is an absolute favorite around here.

FOR THE CARROT LOAF:

2 large Trader Joe's Organic Carrots of Many Colors, boiled and mashed

⅓ cup water

½ teaspoon Trader Joe's Organic Pure Bourbon Vanilla Extract

1 large egg, beaten

2 tablespoons plus 2 teaspoons unsalted butter, melted

¾ cup Trader Joe's Organic Unbleached All-Purpose Flour

½ teaspoon baking soda

pinch of salt

½ teaspoon ground cinnamon

¼ teaspoon ground allspice

½ cup brown sugar

¼ cup pecan or walnut pieces, plus more for topping (optional)

FOR THE CINNAMON BUTTER CREAM CHEESE ICING:

¼ cup unsalted butter, slightly softened

¼ cup Trader Joe's Cream Cheese, slightly softened

1½ cups Trader Joe's Organic Powdered Cane Sugar

¾ teaspoon ground cinnamon (optional)

2 to 3 teaspoons milk of choice

1. Preheat the oven to 350°F and lightly grease a mini loaf pan with olive oil. In a medium bowl, combine the mashed carrots, water, vanilla extract, egg, and melted butter. Mash thoroughly together using a fork until the butter is blended in. Set aside.

2. In a separate medium bowl, whisk together the flour and baking soda until combined. Then add the salt, cinnamon, allspice, and brown sugar and whisk again. Little by little, add the flour mixture to the carrot mix, stirring as you go. Continue until the dry mixture is fully incorporated into the mashed carrot blend. You will have a slightly lumpy batter. Then stir in the nuts until they are well incorporated.

3. Transfer the batter to the prepared loaf pan and bake on the center rack of the oven for 40 minutes. Check for doneness by inserting a toothpick. If the toothpick comes out clean, the loaf is ready; if not, bake for another 5 to 7 minutes, or until the toothpick comes out clean. Remove from the oven and let stand on a cooling rack for 5 minutes, then remove the loaf from the pan and let cool completely.

4. While the loaf is cooling, combine the butter and cream cheese in a medium bowl. Blend together using your hands until well combined. Then add the powdered sugar, cinnamon, and milk and mix until fluffy. Set in the fridge to chill until the loaf is ready to ice.

5. When the cake has cooled completely, ice it liberally with the cinnamon butter cream icing. Top with the nut pieces, if using. Let the icing set, then slice and serve.

PREP TIME: 13 minutes
COOK TIME: 40 minutes
STANDING TIME: 1 hour
TOTAL TIME: 1 hour 53 minutes

MINI MOCHI PINEAPPLE UPSIDE-DOWN CAKE

It had been a long time since I'd had a pineapple upside-down cake. Then, of course, Trader Joe's Mochi Cake Mix inspired me to create my own twist on this delicious, tropical-themed dessert!

1 (15-ounce) box Trader Joe's Mochi Cake Mix

½ cup Trader Joe's 100% Pineapple Juice, at room temperature

½ cup water, at room temperature

4 tablespoons salted butter, melted

2 large eggs, beaten

6 to 10 canned pineapple rings

¼ cup Trader Joe's Organic Unsweetened Flake Coconut

1. Preheat the oven to 350°F. Lightly grease an 8 x 8-inch square or 8-inch round glass baking pan. In a medium bowl, whisk together the cake mix, pineapple juice, and water until smooth. Then add the melted butter and beaten eggs and whisk until smooth. Set aside.

2. Line the bottom of the pan with the pineapple rings, cutting them in half as needed to cover the space. Sprinkle the shredded coconut on top of the pineapple, then pour the batter evenly into the pan.

3. Bake for 45 to 50 minutes, or until the cake is lightly golden and pulls slightly away from the pan sides. Remove from the oven and transfer to a wire cooling rack. Let cool completely for about an hour, then set a serving plate on top and flip the cake over onto the plate to serve.

PREP TIME: 12 minutes
COOK TIME: 45 to 50 minutes
REST TIME: 1 hour
TOTAL TIME: 1 hour 57 minutes to 2 hours 2 minutes

CHEVRE HONEY BLUEBERRY TARTLETS

If you're game for a creamy, fruity, sweet dessert, try whipping up a batch of these fruity tartlets. They're rich and extremely decadent, so you may not even be able to finish a whole tartlet in a serving. But that just means more for later.

1 Trader Joe's Pie Crust, thawed

1 large egg

1 (5-ounce) package Trader Joe's Chevre with Honey Goat's Milk Cheese

1 tablespoon milk of choice

1 tablespoon Trader Joe's Hawaiian Macadamia Nut Blossom & Multi-Floral Honey

¾ cup canned blueberry pie filling

1. Preheat the oven to 475°F. Lightly grease four 3-inch ramekins or tartlet pans. Divide the pie crust into quarters and press each portion into a ramekin or tartlet pan. Trim off any excess dough. Place in the oven and bake for 12 to 14 minutes, or until the crust is golden brown. Remove from the oven and set aside.

2. While the crusts are cooling, combine the egg, chevre cheese, milk, and honey in a medium bowl. Using an electric hand mixer, beat until smooth and fluffy. Set the filling in the fridge to chill while the tartlet crusts continue to cool.

3. Once the crusts have cooled (about 30 to 45 minutes total), reheat the oven to 350°F. Half-fill each crust with the cheese filling and then top with blueberry pie filling. Place the tartlets in the oven and bake for 10 minutes (place the tartlets on a sheet pan for easier removal). Remove from the oven and let stand for 3 to 5 minutes before serving.

PREP TIME: 7 to 10 minutes
COOK TIME: 22 to 24 minutes
REST TIME: 30 to 45 minutes
TOTAL TIME: 59 minutes to 1 hour 19 minutes

PEANUT BUTTER BALLS

While I can't say that these Peanut Butter Balls are fully healthy (hello, brown sugar!), they are a tasty and mostly healthy treat to enjoy together. They're especially great before heading out for a workout or long walk, as they provide some energy and protein without the hassle of making a protein shake.

1 cup Trader Joe's Oven Toasted Old Fashioned Organic Oats, or more as needed

1 teaspoon baking soda

¼ cup light brown sugar

¼ cup Trader Joe's Creamy Salted Peanut Butter

1 large egg

1. Preheat the oven to 375°F, then line a baking sheet with parchment paper. Place the oats in a food processor or blender bowl and grind until they are powdery, like flour, about 10 to 15 seconds. Pour the ground oats into a medium bowl and add baking soda and brown sugar. Whisk together until all the ingredients are fully incorporated.

2. In a separate bowl, combine the peanut butter and egg. beating with an electric hand mixer until smoothly combined. Slowly shake in the mix of dry ingredients, using a wooden spoon to combine them until a dough forms and all the ingredients are well incorporated. If the dough is too sticky to shape into balls, add another tablespoon of ground oats; repeat until the desired texture is reached.

3. Roll the dough into 1½-inch balls and place on the prepared baking sheet, not touching each other. Press them down just enough to keep them in place for baking. Bake for 12 to 15 minutes, or until golden brown, then remove from the oven and immediately place on a tea towel to cool completely before serving. This recipe makes about 4 to 6 balls.

PREP TIME: 10 minutes
COOK TIME: 12 to 15 minutes
TOTAL TIME: 22 to 25 minutes

GLUTEN-FREE COCONUT MOCHI CAKE DONUTS

I'm all about coconut, mochi, and cake donuts, so when I came across Trader Joe's Mochi Cake Mix, I knew I had to experiment. The result is a new favorite sweet treat we enjoy on our date nights.

FOR THE MOCHI CAKE DONUTS:

1 (15-ounce) box Trader Joe's Mochi Cake Mix

1 cup water, at room temperature

4 tablespoons salted butter, melted

2 large eggs, beaten

FOR THE COCONUT GLAZE:

¾ cup Trader Joe's Organic Powdered Cane Sugar

1 tablespoon milk of choice, or more as needed

½ teaspoon coconut extract

¼ cup Trader Joe's Organic Unsweetened Flake Coconut

SPECIAL EQUIPMENT: DONUT PAN

1. Preheat the oven to 350°F. Spray a donut pan with cooking spray and set aside. In a medium bowl, whisk together the cake mix and water until smooth. Then add the melted butter and eggs, whisking until smooth. Transfer the mixture into a piping bag or a plastic ziplock bag with a tip cut off one corner.

2. Pipe the mixture into the pan, filling each donut ring about two-thirds full. Set the pan in the oven and bake for 7 to 10 minutes, or until the donuts are golden brown. Remove from the oven and transfer to a wire cooling rack to cool for about 15 to 20 minutes. Repeat until all the batter is used; this makes 8 to 10 doughnuts.

3. While the donuts are cooling, combine the powdered sugar, milk, and coconut extract for the glaze in a medium bowl. Mix until smooth, then stir in the shredded coconut. If the glaze seems a little thick, add another ½ teaspoon milk; repeat until the desired texture is reached. Once the donuts are cool, dip each one into the glaze. Let the glaze set for about 25 minutes then serve. Store leftovers in an air-tight container on the counter or in cupboard.

PREP TIME: 15 minutes
COOK TIME: 7 to 10 minutes
REST TIME: 15 to 20 minutes
TOTAL TIME: 37 to 45 minutes

HOMEMADE STRAWBERRY POMEGRANATE ICE CREAM

While I'm all about easy desserts, especially when it comes to ice cream, I'm also a huge fan of fruit-flavored ice cream that you often can't find at the store. If you're like me, you'll love this sweet and tart ice cream made from frozen strawberries and pomegranate juice.

¼ pound frozen strawberries, thawed

¼ cup Trader Joe's Organic 100% Pomegranate Juice

½ cup cold heavy whipping cream

½ cup sweetened condensed milk

1. Before starting, place a freezer-safe loaf pan in the freezer for one hour. After the pan has chilled, pulse the strawberries and pomegranate juice together in a food processor until they are combined into a thick, spreadable texture.

2. Using a mixer on medium-high speed, whip the heavy whipping cream until firm peaks form. Pour the fruit mixture into a medium mixing bowl and fold in the whipped cream, about ½ cup at a time, until the cream is well blended into the mixture. Then add the sweetened condensed milk and stir until completely incorporated.

3. Pour the mixture into the chilled pan, and cover, and freeze for about 6 hours before serving.

PREP TIME: 10 minutes
REST TIME: 7 hours
TOTAL TIME: 7 hours 10 minutes

PEPPERMINT HOT CHOCOLATE ICE CREAM SUNDAES

For me, the perfect sundae combines chocolate and mint in all their deliciousness. Having a little zing from sea salt doesn't hurt, and, in fact, it brings out the flavor just a bit more. Pour on some hot fudge syrup, and you win at dessert!

FOR THE PEPPERMINT HOT CHOCOLATE FUDGE SYRUP:

½ tablespoon unsalted butter

¼ cup 1% milk

½ cup plus 1 teaspoon Trader Joe's Peppermint Hot Chocolate mix

FOR THE SUNDAES:

2 to 4 Trader Joe's Sea Salt Brownie Bites

1½ cups Trader Joe's Mint Chip Ice Cream

2 dollops whipped topping

peppermint hot chocolate fudge syrup (directions above)

2 maraschino cherries

1. To make the fudge syrup, place the butter in a small saucepan over medium heat and pour in the milk. Stir constantly until the butter melts, about 2 minutes. Then stir in the hot chocolate mix, a little at a time, until smooth. Reduce the heat to low and cook for 5 to 8 minutes, stirring constantly, until the sauce starts to thicken. Remove from the heat and immediately serve over the ice cream.

2. To assemble the sundaes, place the brownie bites (whole or crumbled) in two large bowls or sundae boats and scoop the ice cream on top. Next add the whipped topping then pour on the Peppermint Hot Chocolate Fudge Syrup. Finish off each sundae with a cherry. Serve immediately.

....

Tip: If this sundae sounds too minty for your taste, you can use vanilla or chocolate ice cream instead of the mint chip ice cream.

....

PREP TIME: 3 minutes
COOK TIME: 9 to 11 minutes
TOTAL TIME: 12 to 14 minutes

ICED VEGAN CHIA PUDDING

For a quick, easy, and healthy dessert to share, try this spicy, icy twist on chia pudding. It takes just a couple of minutes to prepare and only an hour to freeze before it's ready to enjoy.

4 tablespoons Trader Joe's Organic Chia Seeds

⅔ cup Trader Joe's Organic Almond Beverage (Unsweetened Original)

½ teaspoon Trader Joe's Organic Date Syrup

½ teaspoon vanilla extract

1. Combine all the ingredients in a freezer-safe container with a lid. Thoroughly mix together with a spoon, then seal and refrigerate for 20 minutes.

2. Move the container to the freezer for an hour, or until the pudding partially hardens and ice crystals start to form. Divide into two bowls and serve immediately.

PREP TIME: 5 minutes
REST TIME: 1 hour 20 minutes

Beverages for Two

- ICED MATCHA BUBBLE TEA
- ICED ENGLISH BREAKFAST LATTES
- VEGAN-FRIENDLY CREAMY BLENDED ICED MATCHA LATTE
- CREAMY PEPPERMINT HOT COCOA LATTES
- ICED CREAMY POMEGRANATE CHERRY COFFEES
- BLUEBERRY SENCHA GREEN TEA SMOOTHIES
- CARROT ORANGE SMOOTHIES
- POMEGRANATE MANGO SMOOTHIES
- SWEET-TART CHERRY FIZZ
- SPARKLING WATERMELON MOCKTAIL
- DECADENT SPARKLING APPLE CIDER FLOATS

ICED MATCHA BUBBLE TEA

Ever since my first bubble tea, I've been in love with these tapioca pearls and their unique and fun texture. Most of us don't know how to make bubble tea at home without a special kit, but you just have to be able to find the bubbles (check online) and then use some delectable ingredients with them.

6 cups water, divided

2 tablespoons tapioca pearls of your choice (may be called boba)

4 teaspoons Trader Joe's Organic Date Syrup, divided

2 cups ice cubes

¾ cup Trader Joe's Non-Dairy Oat Creamer

1¼ cups milk of choice

2 tablespoons Trader Joe's Matcha Green Tea Powder

1. Add 4 cups water to a small saucepan and turn the heat to medium-high. When the water boils, after about 7 minutes, drop in the tapioca pearls and stir with a wooden spoon. As soon as the tapioca pearls rise to the top (it should take about 4 minutes), remove the pan from the heat and drain.

2. Pour 2 cups cold water into a small bowl and immediately add the pearls. Let stand for about 2 minutes, then drain and transfer the pearls to another small bowl. Drip 2 teaspoons of the date syrup over them and mix until the syrup is absorbed. Cover and place in the fridge.

3. After the pearls have chilled for about 20 minutes, pull out your blender. Add the ice cubes to the blender jar, then the creamer, milk, matcha powder, and remaining 2 teaspoons date syrup. Pulse for 1-second bursts for about 30 seconds. If the mixture is still thick, pulse several more times until the desired thickness is reached.

4. Remove the tapioca pearls from the fridge and divide them evenly between two tall glasses. Pour in the matcha-ice mixture and serve immediately.

Tip: If you think you'll repeat this recipe regularly, you may want to look online for boba straws.

PREP TIME: 5 minutes
STANDING TIME: 20 minutes
COOK TIME: 11 minutes
TOTAL TIME: 36 minutes

ICED ENGLISH BREAKFAST LATTES

For a morning pick-me-up on a hot summer day, this Iced English Breakfast Latte is a favorite in our household. You get all the caffeine of the tea without all that steam.

2 cups water, heated to near-boiling

2 teabags Trader Joe's English Breakfast Tea

½ cup Trader Joe's Non-Dairy Oat Creamer

½ cup Trader Joe's Coconut & Almond Milk Creamer (Vanilla)

1 teaspoon Trader Joe's Fleur de Sel Caramel Sauce

2 cups ice

1. Set water in a tea kettle over medium heat for 5 to 6 minutes, not letting it quite boil. Then remove from the heat and pour 2 cups hot water into a heat-resistant container. Immediately add two English Breakfast tea bags. Cover the container and place in the fridge for 6 hours or overnight.

2. After the chilling period, remove the tea bags and pour the tea into the bowl of a blender. Add the oat creamer, almond milk creamer, and caramel sauce and pulse for 10 seconds, or until thoroughly blended. Pour the mixture over the ice in two tall glasses and serve immediately.

PREP TIME: 5 minutes
COOK TIME: 6 minutes
SREST TIME: 6 hours or overnight
TOTAL TIME: 6 hours 10 minutes or overnight

VEGAN-FRIENDLY CREAMY BLENDED ICED MATCHA LATTE

I am a huge tea fanatic. (You should see my three-tier tea cart!) So any time I have the chance to do some tea-blending or create new tea recipes, I'm all over that. The fact that Trader Joe's has some wonderful tea options makes it even better. I use their basic matcha tea powder for this latte, and it's perfect.

2 cups ice cubes

¾ cup Trader Joe's Coconut Creamer

1¼ cups milk of choice

1 cup water

2 teaspoons Trader Joe's Organic Date Syrup*

2 tablespoons Trader Joe's Matcha Green Tea Powder

*If you prefer less-sweet matcha lattes, use only 1½ teaspoons date syrup.

1. Pour the ice cubes into a blender jar, then add the coconut creamer, milk, water, date syrup, and matcha powder. Pulse for 1-second bursts for about 15 seconds, then increase the pulses to 2 seconds.

2. Repeat the pulses until you have the consistency you want—nearly a minute for a smooth, less "icy" blend, only about 30 seconds for a "chunky" blend.

PREP TIME: 5 minutes

CREAMY PEPPERMINT HOT COCOA LATTES

For a super creamy, cozy treat, cuddle up with these peppermint hot cocoa lattes. They're pretty quick and easy—and absolutely delicious.

1½ cups Trader Joe's Almond Beverage (Unsweetened Original)

½ cup Trader Joe's Coconut Creamer

2 tablespoons Trader Joe's Peppermint Hot Chocolate

2 teaspoons sugar

¼ cup Trader Joe's Semi-Sweet Chocolate Chips

½ teaspoon vanilla extract

whipped cream or peppermint pieces (optional)

1. In a medium saucepan, combine the almond beverage, creamer, hot chocolate mix, and sugar. Place on the stovetop over medium-low heat and whisk the ingredients together until they hit a simmer, about 4 minutes. Then add the chocolate chips and vanilla and whisk again until the chocolate melts and the mix is smooth, about 4 minutes.

2. Remove from the heat and pour the mixture into two large mugs. Top with whipped cream or garnish with peppermint pieces, if desired.

PREP TIME: 3 minutes
COOK TIME: 8 minutes
TOTAL TIME: 11 minutes

ICED CREAMY POMEGRANATE CHERRY COFFEES

I love a tangy fruity drink, and the combination of pomegranate and tart cherry does it every time! But add in some creamer and ice and you've got the perfect sweet and tart pick-me-up for any time of the day.

2 cups ice cubes

1 cup Trader Joe's Cold Brew Coffee (Ready to Drink)

½ cup Trader Joe's Organic 100% Pomegranate Juice

½ cup Trader Joe's 100% Red Tart Cherry Juice

½ cup Trader Joe's Coconut & Almond Milk Creamer (Vanilla)

1 teaspoon vanilla extract

1 teaspoon Trader Joe's Organic Date Syrup (optional)

1. Add the ice cubes to your blender bowl, and pour the cold brew coffee over them. Next add the pomegranate and cherry juices, followed by the creamer and vanilla. Finally, if desired, add the date syrup.

2. Pulse for 10 to 15 seconds for a thicker drink, 30 seconds for a thinner, smoother drink. Pour into two tall glasses and serve immediately.

PREP TIME: 5 minutes
COOK TIME: 5 to 6 minutes
TOTAL TIME: 6 hour 10 minutes

BLUEBERRY SENCHA GREEN TEA SMOOTHIES

Ever since I discovered the benefits of drinking green tea daily, I've been obsessed with this beverage. It didn't take much to get my husband hooked, either. But sometimes you want more than just a mug of green tea to get you going in the morning. Sometimes you need some oomph in that drink. These green tea smoothies offer that and more.

2 cups near-boiling water

2 teabags of Trader Joe's Organic Sencha Tea (Japanese Green Tea)

2 cups ice cubes

2 cups blueberries

2 cups Trader Joe's Organic Baby Spinach

1 cup Trader Joe's Non-Dairy Oat Creamer

2 teaspoons vanilla extract

2 teaspoons Trader Joe's Organic Date Syrup (optional)

1. Set your teakettle over medium-high heat and let the water heat for 5 to 6 minutes but avoid going to a full boil. Pour 2 cups of the hot water into a heat-resistant container with the sencha teabags. Let steep for 15 minutes in the fridge.

2. After the tea has steeped and cooled, remove the teabags. Then combine all the ingredients in the blender bowl—first the ice cubes, then the tea, blueberries, spinach, creamer, vanilla, and date syrup, if using. Cover and pulse for 30 seconds or until smooth.

3. Pour the smoothies into two tall glasses and serve immediately.

....
Tip: If the smoothie mixture is a bit thick, add more creamer a tablespoon at a time to thin it out.
....

PREP TIME: 5 minutes
COOK TIME: 5 to 6 minutes
REST TIME: 15 minutes
TOTAL TIME: 25 to 26 minutes

CARROT ORANGE SMOOTHIES

A good nickname for this drink would be the "all things orange" smoothie. My husband and I adore orange fruits and veggies combined in this super tasty, highly nutritious drink.

1 cup ice cubes

4 Trader Joe's Yellow Cling Peach Halves in White Grape Juice

1 orange, peeled and seeded, broken into sections

1 cup Trader Joe's 100% Organic Carrot Juice

¼ cup Trader Joe's 100% Mango Juice from Carabao Mangoes

1. Combine all the ingredients in the bowl of a blender—first the ice cubes, then the peach halves, orange, carrot juice, and mango juice. Pulse together for 30 seconds for a smooth blend.

2. Pour into two large glasses and serve immediately.

PREP TIME: 5 minutes

POMEGRANATE MANGO SMOOTHIES

Tropical fruit smoothies are always winners in this household, so combining some of the amazing ingredients from Trader Joe's was a no-brainer. Using pomegranate juice, acai purée, fresh mangos, and ice, you can create a simple and delicious healthy treat in no time.

2 cups ice cubes

1 cup diced fresh mango

1 cup Trader Joe's Organic 100% Pomegranate Juice

1 (13.5-ounce) can Trader Joe's Coconut Milk

1 (99-gram) packet Trader Joe's Unsweetened Organic Açaí Puree, thawed

1. Combine all the ingredients in your blender bowl—first the ice cubes, then the mango pieces, pomegranate juice, coconut milk, and acai purée. Pulse together for 30 seconds or until blended to the desired texture.

2. Pour into two tall glasses and serve immediately.

PREP TIME: 6 minutes

SWEET-TART CHERRY FIZZ

You only need a few ingredients for this simple cherry fizz. It's the perfect non-boozy romantic drink for a relaxed evening together.

¼ cup Trader Joe's 100% Pineapple Juice

1¼ cup Trader Joe's 100% Red Tart Cherry Juice

½ cup Trader Joe's Sparkling Strawberry Juice Beverage

maraschino cherries, to taste

1 cup ice cubes (optional)

½ cup whipped cream (optional)

1. Pour the three juices into a pitcher or jar and stir with a wooden spoon. Remove the stems from the maraschino cherries.

2. Half-fill two glasses with the ice cubes, if using, and then drop several maraschino cherries (to taste) into each glass. Pour the juice trio over the ice and top with a dollop of whipped cream, if desired. Serve immediately.

PREP TIME: 5 minutes

SPARKLING WATERMELON MOCKTAIL

All summer long, we bring home a watermelon to enjoy every single week. But what happens when autumn and winter come? We freeze watermelon purée during the summer, then thaw it out in the fridge and combine it with some Trader Joe's ingredients for a fruity mocktail to enjoy at any time of the year.

2 cups chilled watermelon purée

2 tablespoons Trader Joe's Organic Reduced Sugar Raspberry Preserves

12 ounces Trader Joe's Watermelon Lemonade Sparkling Water

1. Set out two tall glasses. First add the watermelon purée, about half for each glass. Then put in the raspberry preserves, and finally fill the glasses the rest of the way with the watermelon lemonade, leaving just a little room at the top.

2. Mix the drinks with a straw only enough to swirl the ingredients together, then enjoy!

PREP TIME: 5 minutes

DECADENT SPARKLING APPLE CIDER FLOATS

For a unique treat that serves as both dessert and drink, Trader Joe's Sparkling Apple Cider offers plenty of sweet goodness on its own. But being a huge fan of ice cream floats, I found a way to really crank up the "dessert" part. Enjoy this decadently sweet treat that we love to share on a romantic evening.

2 cups Trader Joe's Sparkling Apple Cider

1½ cups vanilla ice cream

1 tablespoon milk of choice

2 teaspoons ground cinnamon

2 teaspoons apple butter

½ cup whipped cream (optional)

1. Chill the sparkling cider in the refrigerator for 6 to 8 hours. In a small bowl, combine the ice cream, milk, ground cinnamon, and apple butter. Using the milk to soften and blend the ice cream, mix well small spatula or wooden spoon until the ingredients are fully integrated. Place in a freezer-safe container with a lid and freeze for 6 to 8 hours.

2. After the cider has chilled and the ice cream has refrozen, divide the ice cream evenly between two glasses. Spoon 1 teaspoon of apple butter into each glass. Pour in the sparkling cider, then top with whipped cream if desired. Serve immediately.

PREP TIME: 10 minutes
REST TIME: 6 to 8 hours
TOTAL TIME: 6 hours 10 minutes to 8 hours 10 minutes

Conversions

MEASURE	EQUIVALENT	METRIC
1 teaspoon	--	5.0 milliliters
1 tablespoon	3 teaspoons	14.8 milliliters
1 cup	16 tablespoons	236.8 milliliters
1 pint	2 cups	473.6 milliliters
1 quart	4 cups	947.2 milliliters
1 liter	4 cups + 3½ tablespoons	1000 milliliters
1 ounce (dry)	2 tablespoons	28.35 grams
1 pound	16 ounces	453.49 grams
2.21 pounds	35.3 ounces	1 kilogram
325°F/350°F/375°F	--	165°C/177°C/190°C